A Step-by-Step Guide to Creating a

KITCHEN
GARDEN

A Step-by-Step Guide to Creating a

KITCHEN GARDEN

SMITHMARK

CLB 4541
© 1996 CLB Publishing

This edition published in 1996 by SMITHMARK Publishers,
a division of U.S. Media Holdings, Inc.,
16 East 32nd Street, New York NY 10016
SMITHMARK books are available for bulk purchase for sales promotion
and premium use. For details write or call the manager of special sales,
SMITHMARK Publishers, Inc.
16 East 32nd Street, New York,
NY 10016; (212) 532-6600

Produced by CLB Publishing
Godalming Business Centre
Woolsack Way, Godalming, Surrey, UK

ISBN 0-8317-7599-8
Printed in Singapore
10 9 8 7 6 5 4 3 2 1

Credits

Edited and designed: Ideas into Print
Step-by-step photographs: Neil Sutherland
Typesetting: Ideas into Print and Ash Setting and Printing
Production Director: Gerald Hughes
Production: Ruth Arthur, Sally Connolly, Neil Randles,
Karen Staff, Jonathan Tickner

Contributing Authors

Peter Blackburne-Maze, Yvonne Rees, Rosemary Titterington

*Half-title page: Borage attracts pollinating insects to the garden,
thus improving yields of strawberries and other fruit.
Opposite title page: A bunch of dahlias fresh from
the garden will bring vibrant color to the house in the fall.
Title page: With their many shapes, sizes and colors,
pumpkins and squashes are decorative as well as edible.
Left: Sweet peas fill the air with their heady scent in summer.
Deadhead them regularly to keep them flowering.
Right: 'King of the 'Pippins' is an ideal apple variety
for the garden. Its creamy white flesh is firm and juicy.*

CONTENTS
VEGETABLES AND FRUIT

Above: For best results, pick dwarf French beans when they are young.

Below: Consider taste and yield when choosing apple varieties.

Above: Peach and plum trees can be fan-trained against a wall or fence.

CONTENTS
HERBS AND FLOWERS

Below: Many herbs are easy to propagate from healthy cuttings.

Above: Basil is a superb, aromatic herb with many culinary uses.

Below: Plant annual flowers for bright color in the garden all summer.

Part One
GROWING VEGETABLES

Anyone who has grown their own vegetables will know the pleasure and satisfaction involved, especially when they are sitting on a plate in front of you. It is also extremely cost effective and, what is more, it takes you outdoors and gives you exercise. If you are a newcomer to the subject, there are a few things to consider. For example, which vegetables are you are going to grow and how large an area are you prepared to devote to them? Clearly this will be governed by the size of your garden and how much you like vegetables. As a rule, it is best to avoid crops such as maincrop potatoes and maybe sprouting broccoli that take up a lot of space and/or that remain in the ground for a long time. On the other hand, new potatoes are particularly valuable; one row takes up very little room and new potatoes straight from the garden taste quite unlike any other. Peas and beans are also good value where space is limited, as they crop over a long period. Other worthwhile choices are the winter and early spring vegetables, such as spring greens and spinach beet, which are ready when vegetables in the shops are at their most expensive. Any vegetables that are expensive to buy are always worth growing and so are any that you like but that are difficult to find in shops. Having made these preliminary decisions, the first job is to get the soil into a suitable condition for growing vegetables. This means having the right tools, including a line and dibble for planting out seedlings. Now you are ready to embark on an enjoyable and rewarding venture.

Left: A flourishing vegetable garden. Right: An eggplant (aubergine) with its starry flowers.

Digging the soil

Just as plowing is the farmer's way of moving the soil deeply in preparation for shallower cultivations and seed-sowing, digging is the basic cultivation of the gardener. You must dig any ground that is being cultivated for the first time or that has just been cleared of an old crop. A spade is the normal tool used for digging, but on heavy ground, a strong fork is much easier to use and just as effective. The choice depends on how well the soil holds together. If it falls through the prongs of a fork, then you should use a spade instead.

There are several reasons for digging. The main one is to break up the soil so that excess water can drain away and roots can penetrate in their search for water and nutrients. As the ground is broken up, air is able to reach down into it so that the roots can 'breathe'. Digging also creates a suitable tilth for sowing or planting. When you dig cultivated ground, you bury any existing weeds and weed seeds, which reduces the competition that faces new young plants in their all-important first weeks. Digging is also the most thorough and reliable way of burying bulky organic matter, such as garden compost, that is vital if the soil is to 'live' and support good crops.

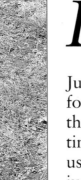 *When single digging a plot of land, use a line to mark out the position of the first trench. The trench should be 9-10in(23-25cm) wide.*

2 *Using a spade, scrape the surface rubbish and weeds off the marked area to give a clean surface. Work your way along in a methodical way.*

3 *Dig out the soil to a full spade's depth and barrow it away to the far end of the plot, where it will be used to fill in the final trench.*

4 *After digging out the trench, clean out the loose earth in the bottom. The trench is now ready to receive the soil from the second trench.*

Using a fork

A fork has two main uses in preparing the soil. It is much easier to use than a spade when digging heavy clay soil and it does a splendid job when you want to break down land that has already been dug. For this, use the back of the fork to break up the clods into a finer tilth. (See page 18 for more details.)

5 If there is not much debris on the surface, turn the soil from the second trench over and forward into the first trench without any scraping.

6 If there are any remains of the previous crop on the surface, be sure to turn each spadeful of soil over completely to bury the rubbish.

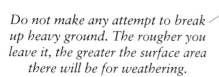

Do not make any attempt to break up heavy ground. The rougher you leave it, the greater the surface area there will be for weathering.

7 Keep working backwards down the plot, scraping if necessary and turning the soil over and forwards into the previous trench as before.

8 Always keep the trench open and clear so that there is enough room to accommodate the next 'row' of soil excavated from the previous trench.

9 Fill the final trench with the earth that was dug out from the first one. If digging a vegetable plot in the fall, leave it to weather until spring.

Below: A fork is one of the most useful tools for breaking down previously dug soil into a tilth suitable for sowing or planting. Do not dig, but knock the clods apart with the back of the fork.

Basic cultivation

In order to grow worthwhile crops, you need at least a basic knowledge of soil cultivation and the tools required to carry it out. As well as a spade and fork (see pages 16-17) you will need a rake to break down the soil surface still further before sowing seeds. When sowing seeds or planting out seedlings, always use a garden line; never rely on drawing out a straight line by eye. Once the plants are growing, they will inevitably be challenged by weeds. The cheapest way of dealing with these is to hoe them out, using either a Dutch or a draw hoe. Never try to cultivate the ground when it is wet enough to stick to the tools and always clean your tools after use. All garden tools can be made of either ordinary or stainless steel. Stainless steel costs more, but does not go rusty. As a general rule, always buy the best tools you can afford; the better they are, the longer they will last.

If the soil conditions are not suitable for the plants you want to grow, your results will be poor. Within the soil the most important material is the organic matter. In nature this comes from decomposed vegetation, but in the garden you must add it in the form of garden compost or farmyard manure. Normal levels of organic matter contain only small amounts of the essential plant foods, so you will need to add these in the form of fertilizers. Under average garden conditions, add both bulky organic matter and plant foods to the soil at least once a year for it to remain in a suitable state for plants to grow well.

Above: After breaking down the clods with the back of a fork, you can make the tilth even finer in preparation for sowing by raking the surface of the soil backwards and forwards.

Food and water

Below: Apply a granular fertilizer to the ground before sowing or planting. Long-standing crops, such as runner beans, will need more feed once they start cropping.

Above: The Dutch hoe is very useful for removing weeds amongst the vegetables. Use it shallowly when the soil is dry and the weeds are small. Killing weeds is a top priority.

Above: The same principles apply to the draw hoe. Catch the weeds in good time, otherwise they will soon be competing with the crop for water, nutrients and space.

Above: Rake in fertilizers after applying them so that they dissolve and move down into the soil more quickly. You can use either organic or, as here, inorganic feeds.

Below: During very dry periods , use liquid feeds in place of granular ones. The plants use the food instantly and also get some water.

Above: Most vegetables will require additional water in the summer. The best irrigation systems are trickle or perforated hoses, as the water is applied where it is needed.

Left: To grow vegetables on heavy soil, create semi-permanent beds 4ft(1.2m) wide. You can walk between the beds and thus avoid treading on the crops.

Right: Inter-cropping makes excellent use of growing space. The lettuces will be long gone by the time the sweetcorn needs the room to grow.

Below: All being well, your vegetable garden should look like this by midsummer. Not a weed in sight and everything growing away.

Making garden compost

Garden compost is one of the most common and effective forms of bulky organic matter that you can add to the ground, and it is also the cheapest. It is made from plant remains that are continually becoming available in every garden, including weeds, spent vegetables, lawn mowings, hedge clippings, flower stalks, leaves and soft prunings. You can also add sawdust, straw and hay, pet litter and bulky animal manures. Household waste, such as potato peelings, cabbage leaves, old cut flowers and tea leaves and a host of other things can all be added to make good garden compost. All these items are of a vegetable origin; never add anything of a meaty nature. The secret of making good garden compost is to use a good mixture of raw materials: plenty of soft vegetation together with a high proportion of woodier things. Autumn flower stalks, woody prunings, cabbage and other brassica stalks are all first-rate, but be sure to chop them up first with a spade or, better still, shred them mechanically. The choice between a compost heap or composting bin rests largely on the amount of raw material available. If there is plenty, a heap is better. However, where raw material is limited, bins are better. Small heaps never make good compost. Ideally, fill up bins in one operation; they quickly heat up and make the best compost.

1 When starting a new heap or bin, try to arrange it so that the first batch of material is coarse and woody, such as these rose prunings. It ensures that the heap will have good drainage and aeration.

2 Keep adding more coarse material until you build up a foundation layer of vegetation about 6in(15cm) deep in the bottom of the bin or heap, once you have firmed it down.

3 Now you can start to add soft materials as well, such as these grass mowings, which will heat up splendidly.

Shredding thorny prunings renders them harmless.

Using a shredder

Some of the best raw materials are woody and cannot go directly onto the compost heap. With a shredder you can make sure that none of this valuable vegetation is wasted. Where it is allowed, you could burn prunings instead and put the ashes on the heap, but this is second best.

Thorny prunings after they have been put through an electric shredder.

Proprietary activators contain nitrogen together with an agent that reduces acidity. The microorganisms prefer an alkaline environment.

4 With the shredded prunings, the heap is about 10in(25cm) deep. This is the time to sprinkle on an activator. It will add nitrogen to the raw materials, helping the microorganisms to break them down into rich garden compost.

5 Continue adding more raw material. These potato tops are soft and full of water so, ideally, you should follow them with rougher material to keep the heap open.

6 Another helping of shredded prunings would be suitable and will also assist the decomposition process by aerating the heap. This, in turn, leads to heating up.

7 With this type of bin you add slats as the heap rises. The gaps are for ventilation. Do not forget to add more activator for every 10in(25cm) or so increase in depth of vegetation.

8 An important part of good composting is to stop the generated heat escaping. Any substantial covering will do this and it will also stop rain from cooling the heap.

9 The result is humus-rich, fibrous garden compost that will improve your soil physically and chemically, either as a mulch or when dug in.

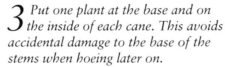

1 Fill 3.5in (9cm) pots with seed or multi-purpose potting mix. Make a small hole and put one seed in each pot, pointed end down, with the top of the seed 1in (2.5cm) below the surface.

Climbing beans

Climbing French and runner beans are two of the most valuable summer vegetables in the garden. They can start cropping in midsummer and, with reasonable upkeep, will carry on until the first fall frosts. Treat both as half-hardy annuals and do not sow them outdoors until mid-spring, by which time the soil will have warmed up and there is little risk of frost. Alternatively, sow them in a greenhouse or frame up to a month earlier, before planting them outside in early summer when all risk of frost has gone. Sow the seeds singly in 3.5in (9cm) pots of sifted soil, seed or potting mixture. Because both vegetables are climbers, provide a support system of strings or sticks, tall enough to allow the beans to climb to about 6ft(2m). The most convenient system is a double row of 8ft(2.5m) canes pushed into the ground. Tie the tops of opposite canes together across the row. Sometimes, runner beans have difficulty in setting the beans. You can improve their chances by spraying the flowers with water most evenings during flowering. Climbing French beans do not have this problem.

2 Push four 8ft(2.5m) canes into the ground about 1ft(30cm) apart and tie into a wigwam. Remove each plant from its pot, holding it gently by the stem.

3 Put one plant at the base and on the inside of each cane. This avoids accidental damage to the base of the stems when hoeing later on.

4 Water the plants thoroughly. If the soil is dry, each plant will need at least one gallon(4 liters) of water to help it grow away quickly.

5 When the plants are about 12in (30cm) tall, tie the main stem to the cane with soft string. After this, the plants will be able to climb up the canes unaided.

6 If the garden does not lend itself to growing vegetables in rows, a block of four wigwams is a useful alternative strategy. These plants have started to flower and look healthy.

7 When plants reach the top of the canes, pinch out the tops. This encourages side shoots to form and keeps the beans at a pickable height.

8 An embryo runner bean amongst the flowers. Encourage good pollination and setting by regular overhead spraying in the evening.

Below: Except for their climbing habit and the varieties, climbing French beans are the same as dwarf French beans. They are not as early-maturing as the dwarf varieties, but carry a heavier crop for a given area.

9 A good crop of runner beans is one of the most valuable vegetables in the garden. They can be eaten at once or frozen for winter use.

Dwarf beans

1 *Being comparatively large, French bean seeds are easy to sow. You can even soak them in water overnight before sowing to soften the coats.*

2 *Sow French beans outdoors in shallow drills or dibble holes 1.5-2in (4-5cm) deep, with the seeds planted 2-4in (5-10cm) apart.*

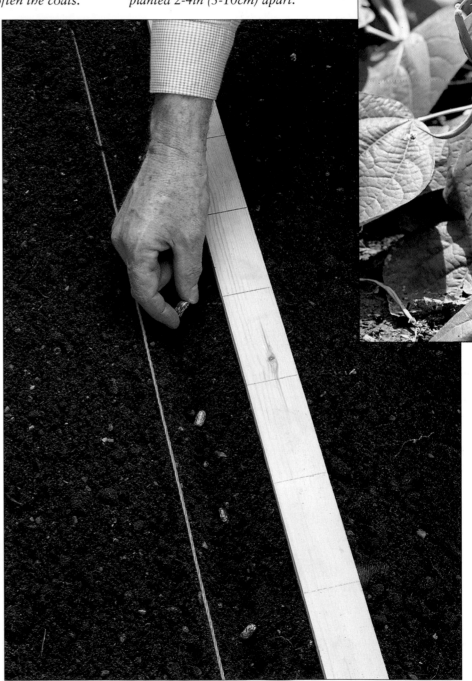

Dwarf French beans are one of the first spring-sown vegetables to mature in the summer. They are usually sown before runner beans so that they mature ahead of them. There are two varieties: the traditional ones with fairly flat pods and the modern 'pencil-podded' kind that are stringless and, therefore, good for freezing. Do not sow these fatter varieties until late spring or early summer, when temperatures are higher. Then sow them in succession. The older, flatter varieties, on the other hand, are hardier and more reliable in poor summers. Although dwarf French beans may be sown earlier if cloches or a plastic tunnel are available, they are seldom raised under glass for transplanting outside later on. Although dwarf French beans are not as liable as the climbing sorts to wind damage in exposed gardens, they still do best in a warm and sunny position. The most important thing to remember about all kinds of beans whose whole pods are eaten (as opposed to broad beans, which are shelled) is that they should be picked when still young. If they are left until they reach their maximum size, they will be tough and uneatable. All varieties will freeze well but some are better than others when cooked after thawing. If your main aim is to freeze them for later use, choose varieties that are specifically recommended for freezing. These will normally be the fatter-podded ones.

3 To maintain this standard of cropping throughout the season, be sure to give the plants plenty of water, especially in a dry year. Dwarf French and dwarf runner beans tend to be quite firmly joined to the plant. When they are ready to harvest, cut them off if necessary, but do not pull them.

Dwarf runner beans

Dwarf runner beans are often grown in small gardens where space is at a premium. They seldom crop as heavily as the climbers, but they still mature over a long period. In fact, although there are dwarf varieties of runner bean, you can keep climbing varieties small and bushy by pinching back all vigorous shoots as soon as you see them. Like their climbing relations, dwarf varieties may be sown under glass for planting outside when the risk of frost has passed. This variety is called 'Pickwick'. The plants are the same size as dwarf French beans.

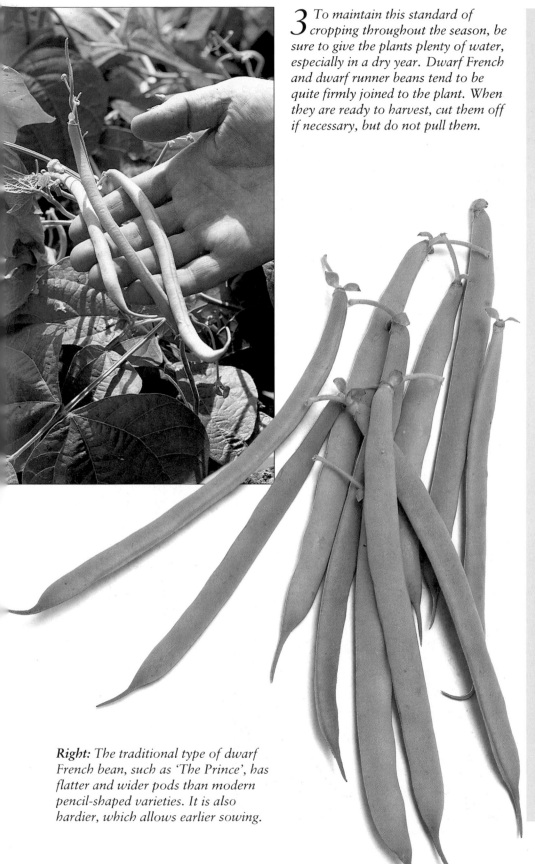

Right: The traditional type of dwarf French bean, such as 'The Prince', has flatter and wider pods than modern pencil-shaped varieties. It is also hardier, which allows earlier sowing.

Broad beans in the ground

Broad beans are one of the hardiest and most easily grown vegetables and the first that many children grow. There are two main types of broad bean: those that you sow in late fall (Aquadulce type) and those that are best left until the late winter or early spring (Windsor and Longpod types). There are now dwarf varieties, which are particularly good for growing in small gardens or even in containers, such as growing bags. The advantages of fall sowing are that the plants crop a little earlier in the summer and are less likely to be attacked by blackfly (the black bean aphid). Another way to discourage blackfly is to nip out the tops of the plants when the bottom flower truss has set beans. You can cook the tops like spinach and these make a pleasant, if not exciting, change. Broad beans (except the dwarf varieties) grow into tall plants; most will reach 3-5ft(90-150cm) and therefore need support. The simplest method is to drive in a stout pole at the corners of each block of plants and stretch twine around them. This prevents the plants being blown about and also makes them easier to pick. The first beans will mature in early summer; never be tempted to wait until the beans within the pods are becoming large. Always pick them when they are still small and tender.

1 Sow the seeds singly in holes or in drills 1.5-2in(4-5cm) deep. Allow 18in(45cm) between the rows. Use a garden line to make the row straight.

2 Plant the seeds about 9in(23cm) apart. Use a trowel, which you have already measured, to determine where the next seed should go in.

3 Beans sown in early winter benefit from weather protection in early spring when they are growing again. Cloches also advance the crop.

4 All broad beans need support once they are 12in(30cm) tall. Run garden twine, looped around canes, around the whole group of plants.

5 Once the lowest flowers on the stem have formed little beans, nip out the plant tips. This directs the plant's energy into bean formation.

6 Only remove the tip of the stem, leaving developing flowers intact to produce beans. Nipping out also discourages the attentions of blackfly.

Above: The reward of attentive gardening: a fine crop of beans for immediate use or for freezing. Do not let them become tough and black-eyed.

7 The young pods are growing well and filling nicely. Do not allow the plants to run short of water and treat them against blackfly if necessary.

Below: The tip of this shoot was not pinched out; it is thin, weak and unproductive, and blackfly have moved in. They feed on the sap and greatly reduce the crop.

27

Broad beans in a tub

Broad beans are so easy to cultivate that there really is no reason at all why you should not grow them, even if you have insufficient space in the garden, as they make splendid plants for growing in containers of all sorts on a sunny patio. The main thing to remember is that you must stick to the dwarf-growing varieties. These are short and sturdy and generally need no support, whereas the normal tall ones do. Choose 'The Sutton' for this type of gardening. The other important point is that you must never grow broad beans under cover once they are more than about 4in(10cm) tall. Any extra warmth will draw them up, so that very soon they become leggy and topple over. Make sure you keep them outdoors, so that the flowers are adequately pollinated by bees.

Because the dwarf varieties are not sufficiently hardy to withstand the winter outdoors, and will become drawn if grown in any heat, you should sow them in the early spring. Unfortunately, this means that they are as susceptible to attacks of blackfly in the summer as are all the other spring varieties (Longpod and Windsor types). Luckily, this pest is easy to control. Besides removing the tip of each shoot once young beans are forming, spray any affected plants with a suitable chemical that will destroy aphids (greenfly and blackfly). Any systemic insecticide will do this, but a spray containing just pirimicarb is more acceptable as it only kills the aphids and nothing else.

1 Fill the container almost full with a good multipurpose potting mixture. Firm it down gently at this stage to prevent later compaction.

2 This is a dwarf variety 'The Sutton'. Sow the seeds individually on the surface about 4in(10cm) apart. Taller varieties are not suitable for containers.

3 Push the seeds into the potting mixture with your finger so that they end up 1.5-2in (4-5cm) deep. Move some soil back over the seeds and firm in gently.

Above: Children enjoy planting the large seeds of broad beans. The seeds are easy to handle and you can expect them all to germinate.

4 Water thoroughly. Do the initial watering in easy stages but do not stop until some drains out of the base.

5 Now you can see the benefits of growing only dwarf varieties. The plants stay short and are much better suited to growing in containers.

6 The young plants growing away well and in flower. When grown outside (cooler than under cover), this variety should need no support.

Garden peas

Garden peas have always been a favorite crop with gardeners. They are relatively easy to grow, are available throughout the summer and are splendid for freezing. Although the true garden pea is the most widely grown, you can also obtain seed for several other types. The petit pois is small-seeded and extremely sweet; with mange tout, or edible-podded, varieties (snap and sugar snap peas), the pods are eaten whole and not shelled. The 'asparagus', or 'winged', pea is also eaten whole, but is very unpealike with its faint asparagus flavor. Peas vary greatly in height and all of them, even the shorter varieties, are easier to manage if you provide them with some support to climb up. This can take the form of twiggy sticks or plastic or wire netting.

The unusual types of pea, such as asparagus pea and mange tout, are sown exclusively in the spring. Gardeners used to make an early sowing of true garden peas in the fall in much the same way as we do with broad beans today. However, there is little advantage in this over the more usual spring sowing. As a rule, the last sowing of garden peas should be no later than early summer, otherwise they are unlikely to mature before the fall frosts arrive. Strangely enough, the later sowings should be of early varieties because these are the quickest to mature.

Many gardeners grow their peas using the trench method. This involves digging out a trench in the winter and filling it with well-rotted garden compost or manure. Put the soil back and sow the peas in this soil later on. This method can result in excellent crops, especially where the natural soil is of a poor quality.

Left: A well-filled pod of fresh peas from your garden - a tasty reward for your efforts. Be sure to keep the plants well watered, though, or they will stop cropping.

1 Pea seeds are nice and large and easy to handle. They look just like dried peas which, in fact, is what they are. Do not sow them too early as they may rot in cold, wet ground.

2 There are several ways of sowing and growing peas, but the simplest is in trenches about 8-10in (20-25cm) wide and 1-2in (2.5-5cm) deep.

3 Scatter the seeds about 2in (5cm) apart. This very arbitrary spacing allows a good, thick stand of plants to develop without being overcrowded.

Below: Cook and eat the whole pod of sugar snap peas when the peas are almost full sized. They can also be used podded, like garden peas.

Above: Mange tout varieties are picked when the pods are still small, flat and tender, with the peas only just visible.

4 Cover the seeds so that they are no more than 2in(5cm) deep. Even coverage is important so that all the seeds germinate more or less together.

5 Firm the soil down with the flat of a rake. This ensures that each seed is in contact with the soil and that the soil stays moist to help germination.

6 Most pea varieties need support. Sticks are the traditional choice, but wire netting is handier, longer lasting and easier to obtain.

Below: Push the little shallot bulbs into the ground 6in(15cm) apart. This will give the resulting cluster of bulbs sufficient room to develop.

Onions and shallots

You can grow onions either from seed or from 'sets'. Sets are the least troublesome way of growing onions. They are the size of baby pickling onions and are planted in the garden normally in mid-spring, although some are suitable for fall planting. Once planted, these miniature onions will grow to the full size. You can sow onion seeds either in late winter in a heated greenhouse for planting out later on or, if you choose the right varieties, you may sow the seeds outdoors in the early fall or in mid-spring. They like a firm and fine seedbed. If you store them well, onions grown one year will keep until the spring of the following year. Dig them up when the tops have died down in the early fall, clean them, dry them off thoroughly and store them in a cold shed. If you keep them indoors, they will start growing and will be useless.

Shallots are very similar to onions but with a milder flavor. They are normally grown from offsets planted outside in late winter or early spring. Once the bulbs are planted, prevent the birds from pulling them out before they have formed roots by threading black cotton along the rows. Each shallot planted will split up into five or six new bulbs. Harvest these in summer when the tops have died down. Onions, shallots and the closely related leeks, garlic and chives, may fall victim to a very unpleasant, damaging soil-borne fungus disease, white rot of onions. This attacks the developing plant at soil level, where it causes the white, feathery, stinking rot to appear. If you spot yellowing plants that have stopped growing, dig them up immediately and burn or throw them away, but never compost them. There is no reliable chemical control for white rot, but do not grow susceptible vegetables in that position for several years.

Above: To grow onions from sets plant them so that just the extreme tip is showing. If there is much more on view, birds will pull them up.

Below: A crop of good-sized 'Kelsae' onions in the making. They thrive on this firm, sandy ground and may even achieve a record-breaking size.

Right: Shallots (at left) and onions like the same growing conditions, so make good companions. Here, both are flourishing in early summer. Shallots were traditionally planted on the shortest day and harvested on the longest one, but this is not critical.

Below: *Onions and related crops, such as leeks, shallots, garlic and chives, have similar-looking seeds and seedlings. Label the rows straight after sowing to avoid any confusion.*

Above: *When growing onions from seed, make sure that they have a firm, fine seedbed. They need this to produce the best-quality bulbs for keeping.*

Right: *Salad, or green, onions are a favorite in summer. They are easy to grow from both spring and fall sowings. Use them before there is much of a swelling at the base. White Lisbon is a first-rate variety.*

Below: *Onions are also highly ornamental and come in a range of colors and sizes. It must be said, though, that the normal golden color has the greatest number of varieties and the highest quality for keeping. The highly colored ones are more of a novelty.*

Among shallots, 'Dutch Yellow' is excellent and 'Hative de Niort' has large, well-shaped bulbs.

Red varieties of onions include 'Red Baron' and 'Red Brunswick'.

There are many golden-skinned onions, including 'Hygro', 'Rijnsburger' and 'Sturon'.

Raising and growing leeks

Although they are not to everyone's taste, leeks do provide a welcome change from the incessant winter cabbages. Like onions, you can sow them either in a heated greenhouse in mid- to late winter or outside in the early to mid-spring. In either event, plant the seedlings outside in their final position when they are about as thick as pencils. To grow those tall, white-stemmed specimens that are the envy of everyone at produce shows, you have to sow early and plant them in the base of a specially dug trench. Later, you wrap newspaper around the young leeks and gradually fill up the trench so that the stems are kept white. To grow normal leeks, however, plant out the seedlings in early to midsummer, but not in trenches. Make holes 6in(15cm) deep and 6in(15cm) apart and, having trimmed the roots back to about 0.5in(1.25cm) long, drop a plant into each hole. No firming in is needed, you merely pour water into the hole. This covers the roots with soil and ensures that the little plants will flourish. Depending on the varieties and when you plant them, you can have leeks ready for digging up from late fall to early spring. The choice ranges from the older 'King Richard', one of the earliest, to the midseason 'Swiss Giant - Albinstar' and the late 'Cortina'. The real leek fanatic can be digging up 'Blauwgroene Winter - Alaska' well into spring.

Leek transplants before and after trimming.

5 *Trimming not only encourages strong new roots, but the smaller leaf area also makes drying out much less likely.*

1 *Sow leek seeds in early spring, either in nursery rows in the garden or in a small pot of seed-sowing mixture in the greenhouse.*

2 *Transplant leeks sown outdoors when they are about as thick as a pencil. Smaller and larger ones do not establish and grow on as well.*

3 *Trim the roots off the transplants, leaving less than 0.5in(1.25cm). Young leeks look very like spring onions and may be used as such.*

4 *Similarly, trim back the tops to leave each transplant about 6-8in (15-20cm) long. This reduces water loss and speeds up establishment.*

6 Make a hole for the roots and drop each transplant in so that a third to half is buried. Do not push the soil back into the hole.

7 Pour water into each hole until it is full up. This ensures that the soil is fully moist and some of it is washed down around the roots.

8 A batch of even and well-grown leeks a few days after transplanting. One or two outside leaves die off, but this is quite normal.

Growing exhibition leeks

1 To grow leeks of exhibition quality, sow two or three seeds in special paper pots in late winter.

2 Push the seeds down 0.5in (1.25cm) and fill in the hole above them with the mixture.

3 Water the pots well and stand them in a warm place in the greenhouse or conservatory or on a sunny windowsill for the seeds to germinate. This will normally take one to two weeks, according to the temperature.

These leeks have been planted further apart and left longer to produce more substantial stems.

Smaller leeks, planted closer together and lifted sooner.

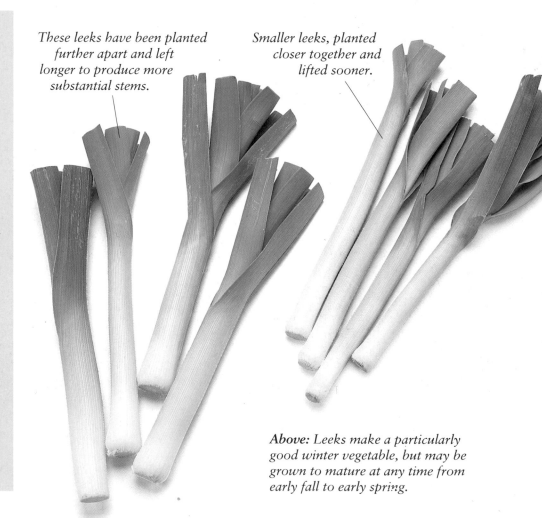

Above: *Leeks make a particularly good winter vegetable, but may be grown to mature at any time from early fall to early spring.*

Sowing lettuces

Lettuces can be raised in two ways, either by sowing them directly into the ground in the place where they are to mature (in situ) or by raising them under protection for planting out when it is warmer. The latter method is mainly used for the hearting varieties - iceberg, butterhead and cos - whereas the leaf varieties, which include many of the exotics, are usually sown in situ. All-year-round lettuces can be a complicated crop, but are quite easy to grow if you have the right conditions and varieties. When sowing lettuces in a greenhouse for planting out later, be sure to stop planting out in late spring and only sow lettuces in situ. If you do continue to plant them out, lettuces usually bolt (produce a flowerhead) because the check to their growth initiates flowering. Furthermore, seed germination is unreliable, or even stops, at temperatures above the mid 70s°F (mid 20s°C). It often pays to sow summer-maturing lettuces in semi-shade, where the temperature is likely to be lower.

Enjoying lettuces all year round

Late spring to early summer:
Sow in heat mid- to late winter, plant outside mid- to late spring.
Early to midsummer:
Sow the seeds in succession outdoors in spring.
Midsummer to mid-fall:
Sow in succession outdoors late spring to late summer.
Early fall to early winter:
Sow outdoors in late summer.
Fall and winter:
Sow in cold frame in early and mid-fall, transplant seedlings to frost-free greenhouse.
Mid- and late spring:
Sow the seed outdoors in late summer and early fall.
Use recommended varieties.

1 Fill a suitable size pot with a good-quality seed sowing or multipurpose potting mix. Gently level and firm the surface of the soil.

Above: *Lettuce seeds are either white or almost black, depending on the variety. If you buy a mixture of varieties, you will often find both colors; do not let this worry you.*

2 To aid seed germination, dampen the soil with a fine-rose before sowing until water runs out of the holes in the base.

3 Sprinkle the seeds evenly and thinly over the surface of the soil. If you sow too thickly, the seedlings will be lanky and weak.

4 Cover the seeds with sifted potting mix. Firm the surface lightly to ensure that the seeds are in contact with the soil.

5 If you prefer to water after sowing, stand the pot in a bowl of water until moisture soaks up to the surface.

6 Cover the pot with a sheet of glass or plastic to maintain a damp atmosphere. Label it and stand it in a warm, but not too sunny, place.

Sowing outdoors

You can sow lettuce seeds directly into well-prepared ground. These rows of seedlings are sufficiently well advanced to be thinned and singled to, say, 10in(25cm) apart. Fill any gaps in the row with the thinnings.

7 At this stage, the seedlings are ready for pricking out. Take out a clump at a time and plant singly into a seed tray filled with potting mixture.

8 Make a dibble hole large enough to take the root system comfortably, put the roots in the hole and firm in the sides so that the seedling is self-supporting.

Pricking out seedlings into individual pots

If you need only a few lettuce plants at a time, prick out the seedlings into individual peat or composition pots. Leave the seedlings in these pots when planting them out to avoid disturbing the root system. Always water thoroughly before planting out.

9 There is no firm rule for spacing out the seedlings; 1.5-2in(4-5cm) is about right.

10 Water the seedlings thoroughly with a fine-rosed watering can. Plant them out after about one month and then start feeding them.

Lettuce varieties

Although we used to consider lettuces as a summer crop, we can now grow and buy them throughout the year. Nor are they just of the traditional kind. The crispheads overtook the softer butterheads in popularity long ago, but we also have the cos varieties, together with the newer 'cut-and-come-again' leaf varieties and the colorful 'exotics'. Not surprisingly, lettuces vary in the planting conditions they require to flourish (see pages 36-37). According to the type and variety, they also vary in their spacing requirements. Space butterheads at 9-10in(23-25cm) apart, with 11-12in(28-30cm) between the rows. Icebergs prefer more room, so allow 15in(38cm) between each plant and between the rows. Cos and leaf lettuces can be planted slightly closer at 14in(35cm) square. It is always best to go by the spacing recommended on the seed packet, but follow these general guidelines if you are in any doubt. A good tip is to plant or thin at half the recommended spacing. Later, you can use alternate plants for an early crop.

Below: The cos is one of the heaviest lettuces. It also takes up a great deal of room, but is first-rate for a large family. 'Lobjoits' is an excellent variety.

Above: The 'exotics' are the latest things in lettuces. They are usually of the 'cut-and-come-again' sort, such as this frilly-leaved 'Lollo Bionda'.

Lettuce varieties

Summer-maturing (outdoors):
Butterhead: 'Avondefiance'
Crisphead: 'Saladin'

Summer leaf lettuce:
'Salad Bowl' and 'Red Salad Bowl', 'Lollo Rossa'

Winter leaf lettuce:
'Winter Density'

In the greenhouse:
Butterhead: 'Novita'
Crisphead: 'Kellys'

Above: Lettuces can be grown all the year round with protection. 'Kweik' is fine in an unheated greenhouse.

Exotic lettuces

The exotics are pretty enough to be grown in flower borders to very good effect. They carry on growing for many weeks; just pull off the leaves as you want them. Hearting varieties, such as the dark red-tinged 'Pablo', are better grown in the vegetable garden, as with these you cut the whole plant as required. They can all be sown where they are to mature and then singled. The 'leaf' varieties tend to have a stronger taste than the hearting ones.

Above: This collection of exotics includes 'Lollo Rossa', 'Lollo Bionda' and 'Red Salad Bowl'. All are easily grown in gardens.

Above: The popular 'Red Salad Bowl' goes well with 'Green Salad Bowl'. Both are 'leaf' lettuces that do not form a heart.

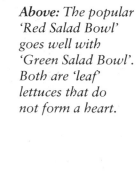

Left: This crisp 'Iceberg' type of lettuce is much heavier and denser than the butterhead sort, with its much softer leaves. There are a great many varieties of each to choose from.

39

Spring and summer cabbages

Fall and winter cabbage varieties take up rather a lot of space and for a considerable length of time, so it is more practical to consider the spring and summer varieties here. Although you would normally think of spring cabbages as being the first to mature in the year, in fact, a sowing of the summer cabbage 'Hispi' in a heated greenhouse in late winter will mature earlier. Harden off the seedlings and plant them outside in mid-spring 18in(45cm) apart when they are large enough. Alternatively, or if you do not have a heated greenhouse, sow the seed outside from early to mid-spring, plant out the seedlings in late spring and eat the result in midsummer. This, of course, would be later than spring cabbages. Successional sowings and later varieties will carry on the cropping season. Spring cabbage and spring greens are the most satisfying of vegetables. The 'greens' are simply immature spring cabbages and they are some of the first vegetables to be ready once the winter is over. The primary crop is spring cabbages, which are sown in mid- to late summer. However, if you transplant the resulting seedlings in early to mid-fall at half the spacing recommended for cabbages, you can cut alternate plants as greens when they are large enough and are touching in the row in spring. Leave the remaining plants to mature into fully fledged spring cabbages. Summer cabbages can be something of a mixed blessing, but just a few can make a welcome change in summer from the normal run of peas and beans. Beware, though, because come the fall, many vegetable gardens are 'wall-to-wall' cabbages and savoys until the winter is over. 'Durham Early' and 'Spring Hero' are good spring cabbages and 'Hispi' and 'Minicole' are recommended as summer varieties. The caterpillars of the large and small white butterflies can be devastating pests. At the first sign of the white butterflies in summer, you should spray the plants with a suitable insecticide, such as permethrin, or a biological one based on *Bacillus thurigiensis*, to avoid problems later on.

1 *Cabbage, cauliflower, Brussels sprouts, etc., have very similar seeds and seedlings. Label the rows straight after sowing or planting out.*

2 *Make a drill, or groove, in the ground about 0.5in (1.25cm) deep using a stick. Be sure to use a line for straightness. Failing this, use a draw hoe but do not go any deeper than is necessary.*

3 *Sow the seeds evenly and thinly so that they produce strong, stocky seedlings that will develop into good plants. If you sow the seed too thickly, the resulting seedlings will be crowded together and drawn.*

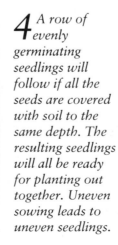

4 *A row of evenly germinating seedlings will follow if all the seeds are covered with soil to the same depth. The resulting seedlings will all be ready for planting out together. Uneven sowing leads to uneven seedlings.*

5 A good way to mark where the plants are to go is to stand a pot at each station. Use a garden line and measuring stick to establish the exact positions for each pot.

This is spring cabbage. The shape has no connection with the time of maturity, but pointed cabbages make the best spring greens.

Anyone would be proud of growing summer cabbages such as this one.

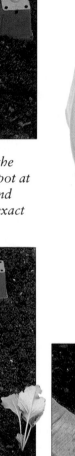

6 You can use a dibble or, as here, a trowel for planting out the young cabbages. Make the hole deep enough for the root system to be vertical or the roots will not grow downwards.

7 Always plant firmly. This ensures that the roots will quickly start growing and the plant soon becomes established without first drying out.

8 A thorough watering is essential, even when the soil is moist. It means that the plant will receive only a slight check. Keep watering if necessary.

9 A beautifully even row of a first-rate summer cabbage, namely 'Hispi'. This variety can also be grown as a spring cabbage by sowing it in a heated greenhouse in late winter.

Squashes and pumpkins

The cucurbit family, to which squashes and pumpkins belong, is a large one that includes marrows, courgettes (zucchini), cucumbers, gourds and melons. Their cultivation dates back about 7000 years. While marrows and cucumbers are common enough in Europe, squashes and pumpkins are far more widely grown in America, though they are spreading fast. As far as gardeners are concerned, there are two distinct types of squashes: summer and winter. Marrows and courgettes are a form of summer squash; pumpkins of winter squash. Although their cultivation is similar, summer squashes are essentially used when they are ready, but winter squashes are sown later and stored, when ripe, for use in winter. Harvest summer squashes well before they are old and tough, but leave winter squashes to mature. As a rough guide, winter squashes need about four months from sowing to maturity; summer squashes, somewhat less. Both may be of either bush or trailing habit. Because of the longer summer required for winter squashes, they are more popular in America than Europe, which favors the summer squash. Raise the plants in the same way as courgettes (page 44) from mid- to late spring sowings under cover and plant them outside as soon as the risk of frost is over in early summer.

Right: Almost all squashes are an odd shape. This 'Golden Crookneck' summer squash is typical.

Onion squashes have a fairly sweet orange flesh. Best baked in the oven.

Right: These winter squashes were matured outdoors before being moved into a greenhouse or conservatory. The ripening process is important as they will only keep if the outer skin is hard and disease-free.

The pajama squash has many seeds and is quite watery. It is fairly tasteless.

The pumpkin can be used in sweet or savory dishes.

The 'Ponca Butternut' has few seeds and a sweet, rich nutty flavor. Ideal for baking and can be served as a sweet dish.

Pumpkins have firm golden flesh surrounding a mass of seeds.

Good varieties

Summer squash: 'Custard White'
'Tender and True'.

Winter squash: 'Butternut'
'Vegetable Spaghetti'
'Hubbard's Golden'
'Table Ace'
'Turk's Turban'

Pumpkin: 'Mammoth'
'Atlantic Giant'
'Crown Prince'
'Cinderella'

Right: *Pumpkin 'Cinderella'. These very decorative pumpkins grow slowly to a large size and develop a flattened top and attractive lobes. The rich flesh is edible or they can be used for ornamental purposes.*

'Turk's Turban' has tough skin and the flesh is best boiled and mashed.

'Sweet Dumpling' squash has the same tasty flesh as 'Delicata'. The skins of both can be eaten.

Below: *The 'Atlantic Giant' pumpkin is one of the varieties that can reach over 500lb(230kg) in weight. They need a long growing season, plenty of room and should be restricted to one fruit per plant to achieve this. They are grown mainly for competition.*

Golden acorn squash. The orange flesh has a potato texture.

'Little Gem' squash. The orange flesh is slightly watery. Inedible skin.

'Delicata' has deliciously sweet, chestnut-flavored golden flesh.

Growing courgettes (zucchini)

Twenty years ago, these vegetables attracted only scant attention, yet today gardeners grow courgettes (zucchini) as though they always have. Grow them in a sunny position and in fertile soil well supplied with bulky organic matter. As they are frost-tender, sow them under cover in mid-spring for planting outside in early summer or outside in late spring where they are to grow.

Courgettes were originally just young marrows. Now there are particularly prolific varieties that will carry on fruiting over a long period. Many will continue bearing even if you leave one or two fruits to develop into marrows. As a rule, though, you should pick over the plants regularly and often to ensure a good succession of courgettes. Try not to let them reach more than about 6in(15cm) long.

The best varieties of courgette (zucchini) are of bush habit; they take up much less room than the trailing type and are perfect for most gardens. Like marrows, pumpkins, squashes and cucumbers, they are half-hardy and even the slightest touch of frost will damage or even kill them. This means that in a cool temperate climate you must sow them and grow on the seedlings in a greenhouse or a sunny room until they are large enough to plant outside after the risk of frost is over.

1 Raise courgettes in individual peat pots. Water well and put them in a plastic bag in a warm place to germinate. When they come through, put in full light.

2 Given warmth, the young plants will grow quickly and are ready for potting on or planting out when a good number of roots are growing through the sides of the peat pot.

3 Leave the top of the rootball 0.5in (1.25cm) above the soil. This helps to prevent collar rot fungus disease, as the vulnerable area is able to dry out.

Put two plants in a standard-size growing bag.

4 A good initial watering is vital for these plants. It also helps prevent red spider mites becoming established; they dislike a damp atmosphere.

5 *A few weeks later, the plants are growing away nicely. Ignore the slight difference in foliage; this is a varietal characteristic and not harmful in any way.*

6 *Courgettes grow very successfully in the ground. Lay perforated black plastic around the plants to reduce mud splash and the risk of disease.*

8 *With the right care and plenty of water, you can have courgettes throughout the summer. Always grow a proper courgette variety; a marrow will not do.*

7 *Pick courgettes regularly. Not all varieties continue fruiting if some are allowed to grow into marrows. The two youngsters on the right are aborting.*

New potatoes

Maincrop potatoes are uneconomical in a small garden, but with the help of some cloches or a plastic tunnel, you could be lifting enough new potatoes for a meal when those in the shops are still very expensive. Plant two rows at the most and preferably just one. Even new potatoes take up a great deal of space; an earthed-up row will be at least 18in(45cm) wide. Even without covering the rows, you can still make the crop come earlier by 'chitting' the seed potatoes (causing them to sprout) in a warm room or greenhouse in late winter. Do not worry about keeping the potatoes in the light in the early stages, but once the shoots start to appear, put them in full light to prevent the shoots becoming drawn. When the soil has warmed up sufficiently (look for seedling weeds) in early to mid-spring, plant the tubers about 1in(2.5cm) below the surface and 12-15in(30-38cm) apart. As soon as the shoots appear, be ready to rake some earth over them if a night frost is likely. In any event, earth them up when the shoots are about 6in(15cm) tall so that all but the topmost leaves are buried. It is from the buried stems that the new potatoes grow. Given reasonable weather, you should have an eatable crop in about 16 weeks. You can also grow new potatoes in large plant pots or tubs, as shown here.

1 To 'chit' potatoes, stand them in a warm, preferably dark, place in small pots or on an egg tray, with the eyes (buds) pointing upwards.

Potatoes that have been chitted will grow away much faster than unchitted ones after planting out. Once the eyes have developed into shoots, be very careful not to damage them or knock them off.

2 Used soil-based potting mixture or some old growing-bag mix is fine for potatoes. New compost can lead to rather too much top growth.

3 Fill the pot or tub with the potting mixture until it is one third to half full. Firm it down gently. This tub is about 18in(45cm) in diameter.

4 Lay in the chitted seed potatoes, leaving 6-8in(15-20cm) between them. This will produce a good crop without overcrowding the potatoes.

5 Cover the potatoes with about 1in(2.5cm) of potting mix and level the surface. There will be enough fertilizer left in the old potting mix.

6 Give the container a thorough watering and stand it in a warm place.

Regular care

The main thing that you must remember when growing potatoes in a sunroom or greenhouse in this way is that the plants are dependent upon you for everything. Make sure that they have enough water and that they do not get too hot. You should not need to feed them, as there will be enough nutrients in the potting mix. If you like, you can move the tub outside, but not until you are sure that there is no risk of frost. The safest time is usually early summer.

9 A fine crop of tasty new potatoes makes all the work worthwhile. Use an early variety; they have the shortest growing season and are therefore ready the soonest. This one is 'Arran Pilot'.

8 It is never easy to be sure, by looking at the tops, when the potatoes are ready for eating. Scrape away the soil to expose a few tubers.

7 A fine display of foliage is the forerunner of a delicious crop. If you have the conditions and can obtain (or save) seed tubers, you can grow potatoes all year round.

Carrots

Carrots are one of the most versatile of vegetables. You can grow them in one form or another throughout the year, from the young pencil carrots that are ready in early summer to the semi-mature roots that can be lifted later in the summer and through the fall. These are followed by the mature vegetables that are stored for use over the winter. Carrots must have a deep and fertile soil that is able to hold plenty of moisture. In particular, you need to grow the early varieties quickly if they are to be tender and tasty. Never grow carrots on land that has just had compost or manure dug in, as they usually produce divided roots. For the earliest crops of tender, young carrots, broadcast the seed, rather than sow it in rows, during early spring. Since the outside temperature will hardly be high enough for germination, use cold frames or lay perforated or slitted clear plastic over the sown seeds as a protection and remove this after about eight weeks.

Good varieties

'Amsterdam': Sow mid- to late winter. Grow under cloches or plastic. Matures early summer.
'Nantes': Sow late winter to mid-spring. Grow in the open. Matures midsummer to early fall.
'Chantenay' and 'Red Cored': Sow mid- to late spring, the crop matures mid- to late fall.
'Autumn King': Sow late spring, matures early winter onwards.

Above: *These maincrop carrot seedlings are ready to be thinned and singled to 1in(2.5cm) apart. Thin them again when they touch. The thinnings are delicious to eat.*

Growing early carrots

1 *Like other vegetable members of the Umberiferae family - parsnip, celery and parsley - carrot seed is slow to germinate.*

2 *Early carrot varieties may be sown broadcast in cold frames or under clear plastic. Sow thinly, rake the seed in and then water.*

3 *Early, frame-grown carrots are pulled at this stage. They are sweet and delicate either cooked or sliced into salads.*

Below: *These gappy rows of carrots are victims of the carrot fly, whose maggots live in the soil and damage or even kill the vegetable's roots.*

Right: *Because the adult carrot flies stay close to the ground, placing a barrier around the rows will stop them reaching the crop.*

Left: *Here, the mesh surrounding the carrots is clearly visible. Mesh is better than plastic sheet, as it allows the air to circulate freely around the carrots.*

Topped and scrubbed maincrop carrots ready for the pot.

Above: *Juicy carrots make a good winter vegetable. Lift them, clean them and store them in net bags in a dark shed.*

Beetroot

Beetroot is one of those vegetables that you either like or loathe; there seem to be no half-measures. Although they are used a great deal for pickling in vinegar, the freshly boiled, skinned roots make a pleasant and different vegetable all the year round. Beetroot is easy to grow as long as you remember that several of the summer varieties are likely to bolt (run to seed) if they are sown too early in the spring. You can buy bolt-resistant varieties to sow in early spring, but mid- to late spring is more usual and always safer. Bolt-resistant varieties are easily the best to grow and they will provide the main crop in late summer and fall. Further sowings in late spring and early summer can be of long beet that you can store like carrots and use during the winter. The simplest way to grow beetroot is in rows 5-6in(13-15cm) apart. Thin and single the plants to the same distance apart within each row as soon as the seedlings touch. Cover the seedlings with netting to protect them from birds.

Below: This is how far apart you should grow beetroot. Any closer and the greater competition slows down growth and toughens the beet.

1 *Beetroot seeds develop in clusters on the plant. In the past, this gave rise to bunched seedlings that had to be singled. Now, seed is available already rubbed (monogerm) from which the seedlings arise singly.*

2 *Using a garden line to be sure of keeping the row straight, take out an even drill 0.8in(2cm) deep in preparation for sowing. You can make the drill with a draw hoe, as shown here, or simply use a stick.*

3 *Sprinkle the seeds thinly and evenly, about an inch (2.5cm) apart. The seedlings will be thinned out later; sowing thinly avoids waste.*

Above: *Be sure to twist the tops off beetroot straight after pulling them. This stops the leaves wilting and absorbing water from the beetroot.*

Below: *This is a fine crop of cylindrical beetroot, but it is still only half-grown. When the vegetables are mature, they can be stored away for use in winter.*

Left: *These beetroot are just the right size for cooking as a fresh vegetable. They could also be pickled in vinegar, but this is usually left for the larger and tougher ones. The single root is a good feature.*

Radishes

Although unrelated to beetroot, radishes also need to be grown quickly so they remain tender with no woodiness. These are summer radishes, but you can also grow winter ones.

51

Sweetcorn

Sweetcorn is the modern descendant of a very ancient plant native to Central America. Not surprisingly, it is more at home in a Mediterranean climate than in a cool temperate one, but given purpose-bred varieties and a good summer, there is every chance of success in reasonably mild regions. The site should be open and must receive plenty of sun. A soil well supplied with garden compost or manure and sufficient lime to correct strong acidity is also necessary. In order to get good results, sweetcorn must have a long growing season. Modern varieties will be ready for picking about four months after sowing. However, you must balance this with having the plants inside and protected while there is still a risk of spring frosts. Sow the seeds, therefore, in a greenhouse in mid-spring or in a cold frame from mid- to late spring. Plant the seedlings out when the risk of frost is over. If you do not have either a greenhouse or cold frame, you can sow the seeds where the plants are to grow outdoors in late spring or early summer. Once established, keep weeds at bay to avoid competition.

When hoeing, be careful not to disturb, and certainly not damage, the surface roots; these are important feeding roots as well as the plant's main support. Provide plenty of water in dry weather. Do not plant traditional and supersweet varieties together, as cross-pollination can affect the quality of the supersweets.

1 The best way of raising young sweetcorn plants is to sow the seeds individually in cardboard tubes filled with seed or multipurpose potting mixture and supported in trays.

2 Place a seed in the top of each tube and press it about 1in(2.5cm) into the mixture. Fill the hole with more mixture and water carefully to avoid washing the seed down.

Sweetcorn varieties

Older varieties, even though many are F1 hybrids, make taller plants than the modern ones and the cobs are coarser and less sweet. These include 'Sunrise', 'Sundance' and the outdated 'Bantam'. The newest varieties are the 'supersweets', so named because of their exceptionally sweet flavor. So sweet are they that you can eat them raw! They also make shorter plants than the older ones. Avoid growing the two types close together as the supersweets are not as good if pollinated by the old varieties.

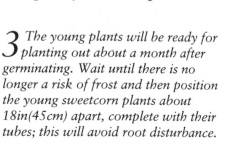

3 The young plants will be ready for planting out about a month after germinating. Wait until there is no longer a risk of frost and then position the young sweetcorn plants about 18in(45cm) apart, complete with their tubes; this will avoid root disturbance.

Left: *Grow sweetcorn plants in blocks rather than rows; this helps the pollination process. These plants are flowering and developing well.*

This is the male part of the plant where the pollen is produced.

These 'silks' are the female part that catch the pollen as it falls from above. Fertilization of the seed follows.

Right: *This semi-mature cob is filling well, but is not quite fat enough to be harvested. The dried up silk is clearly seen; its job completed.*

Right: *Test for maturity by exposing the center of the cob and pushing your thumbnail into a seed. It should be soft but if 'milk' appears, leave it a bit longer.*

Celery

Celery is a vegetable with such a strong and characteristic taste that it is not to everyone's liking. Varieties fall into two distinct groups. The older and traditional kinds are grown in trenches, which are then filled in to blanch (whiten) the stalks. The newer varieties are self-blanching and do not need the trench treatment. Plant these on the surface close together; that is enough to blanch the stems. The soil for celery must be rich in organic matter. This makes it perfectly drained and yet moisture-retentive; just what celery needs. Heavy land is seldom satisfactory unless it is continually improved with bulky organic matter (garden compost, manure, etc.). In addition, slugs are usually troublesome on heavy clay. The best-flavoured celery is still the traditionally trenched sort but modern self-blanching varieties are almost as good and are much easier to grow. Plant these 9-10in (23-25cm) apart in blocks surrounded by wooden planks about 6in(15cm) high to improve the blanching.

Blanching celery

This is a row of trenched celery after its final earthing up. The young plants were set in the trench, enclosed in newspaper, and the trench progressively refilled to its present level.

1 These self-blanching celery plants were pricked out singly as seedlings. They are now at the right stage for planting out.

Left: *Late summer and the closeness of the plants is now apparent. This has kept the stalks pale and tender. The blanket mulch was put down before planting to help retain moisture and suppress weeds.*

Right: *Celery as prepared for sale. The leaf stalks are the edible part and you can eat them raw, either on their own or chopped up as part of a salad. Alternatively, you can enjoy them cooked as an individual vegetable or, again, chopped up and used in stews. A very versatile vegetable.*

2 *Water the plants in well; they will need plenty of water throughout the summer months for quick growth and tender stalks.*

Cut off the leaves straight after lifting. If left on, water evaporates through them and the stalks lose their crispness.

Tomatoes in the ground

Both single stem and bush varieties of tomatoes will grow perfectly satisfactorily in the ground, either in a greenhouse or outside. First, dig the ground deeply and incorporate plenty of well-rotted garden compost or farmyard manure to provide an abundance of the organic matter that is essential for good results. Raise the plants in the usual way in a greenhouse or indoors on a sunny windowsill. Once they are large enough, greenhouse tomatoes can be planted out at any time in the spring, but do not plant outdoor varieties until the risk of frost is over. Plant bush varieties 20in(50cm) apart, disbudded varieties 2-3in(5-7.5cm) closer, and support the plants with a stout stick to help them withstand wind and rain. Probably the greatest disadvantage of outdoor tomatoes is that the season is a good month (two weeks at each end) shorter than for greenhouse crops. You can partly compensate for this in the fall by covering the ground under the plants with straw, cutting the plants loose from the supporting stake and laying them on the straw. Then place large cloches or plastic tunnels over the plants to keep them warmer and drier, thus extending the season. When even this strategy ceases to work, cut off the fruit trusses and bring them indoors to finish ripening. With luck, they should last until early or midwinter.

1 When the first flowers open, plant out the tomato firmly, but gently. Water it in well and tie it to a cane with soft twine.

2 Unless it is a bush variety, remove any side shoots that appear when plants become established.

3 Remove the side shoot with a sharp tweak. Start from the top of the plant and work downwards.

Sowing tomato seeds

1 Tomato seeds vary in size with the variety. Sow them indoors or in a heated greenhouse.

4 Gently cover each seed with more potting mixture. This is a good way of raising a few plants.

Tomato varieties

Some varieties should only be grown under cover, others outdoors. Remember, they are not interchangeable.

Large-fruited: 'Dombito' (for greenhouse cultivation)
Normal: 'Sonatine' (for greenhouse cultivation) 'Red Alert' (for growing outdoors)
Cherry: 'Sweet 100' (for greenhouse cultivation) 'Gardener's Delight' (for growing outdoors)

2 Sow seeds singly in trays of seed or multipurpose potting mix. Put one seed in the center of each cell.

3 Push the seed no more than 0.5in(1.25cm) into the potting mix with the flat end of a pencil.

 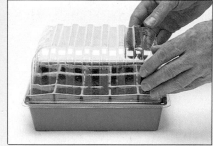

5 Stand the tray in a shallow basin of water until water soaks up to the surface. Drain for 10 seconds or so.

6 Cover the tray with plastic or glass and stand it in a warm place for the seeds to germinate.

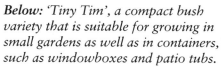

Below: 'Tiny Tim', a compact bush variety that is suitable for growing in small gardens as well as in containers, such as windowboxes and patio tubs.

Below: This 'Marmande' type of tomato is a single stem variety with huge, ribby fruits. The fruits contain little seed and seed pulp.

Above: Towards the end of the season, plants may show signs of magnesium deficiency, usually brought about by high potash feeds. Not a cause for concern.

Below: A well-grown tomato crop is tasty and can save you money, so it is well worth spending time on it.

Tomatoes in a growing bag

One of the best ways of growing tomatoes, in a greenhouse and outdoors, is in a growing bag. Tomatoes are susceptible to root diseases at the best of times and greenhouse plants are especially vulnerable. Growing bags are free of pests and diseases and the plastic isolates plant roots from any diseased soil. Both single stem (disbudded) and bush varieties grow well in bags; raise the plants as described on page 56. Generally speaking, grow one less plant of a bush variety than a disbudded one, because a bush type takes up more room. Follow the general rules for watering growing bags; wait until the surface of the soil has dried out and then give at least a gallon(4 liters) of water at a time. Feeding is not necessary for the first few weeks, but once the first fruits are pea-sized, feed according to the instructions on the bag or the bottle. To allow sun and air to reach the bottom fruits, remove the leaves from the base of the plant up to the lowest truss that has fruit showing red. Tomatoes dislike high growing temperatures, so make sure that the greenhouse is adequately ventilated and shaded. Too much heat leads to excessive water loss and this can cause problems, notably blossom end rot.

3 *Firm the plant gently but adequately into place. Never push the soil down too hard or you run the risk of it becoming waterlogged.*

1 *Never pull a plant from its pot; turn it upside-down, tap the rim on a bench and let the plant drop into your hand. This rootball is full of healthy roots.*

2 *Scoop out a planting hole in the growing bag. This usually means going right down to the bottom to get it deep enough.*

When to plant out tomatoes

The tomato below is too young to plant out. Extra growth induced by putting it into new soil will lead to an unfruitful bottom truss. The tomato at right has the first flower open and is ready to plant out.

4 Put in three plants per bag in a greenhouse. Outdoors, plant four single stem, but only three bush plants per bag.

5 Apply up to 1.5 gallons(6 liters) of water at the first watering. Later waterings can be slightly less.

6 The same growing bag some weeks later. Being a bush variety, the side shoots have not been removed from the plant, so flowers abound with the promise of a good crop.

Above: *The tomatoes on this bush variety are maturing, providing an attractive array of colors from pale green to bright red. Single stem varieties in growing bags in a greenhouse should grow to six or seven fruit trusses high; outdoors expect to ripen four or five trusses. In both cases, nip out the plant at two leaves above the top truss.*

59

Growing sweet peppers

Peppers need a Mediterranean climate to flourish outdoors, but in cool, temperate climates they will really only succeed in a greenhouse, whatever you might read to the contrary. Sweet peppers ripen to a bright red, yellow or black, depending on the variety. However, you can use them before they reach their mature color as long as they are fully grown. Sow the seeds in a heated greenhouse or propagator from late winter to mid-spring and prick out the seedlings singly into small pots of multipurpose potting mixture. If you only want a few plants, sow two or three seeds in a small pot and single the plants to one per pot when they are large enough to handle, remove all but the best seedling in each pot. Plant them in their final fruiting position when the first flowers are visible. The plants normally branch out naturally, but if they have not done so by the time they are 12in(30cm) tall, nip out the growing point. Although the peppers are not fully ripe until they reach their mature color, pick the first few while they are still green to encourage more to form. 'Bellboy' and 'Canape' are good varieties. Between planting out peppers and picking the first fruits, their cultivation is much the same as for tomatoes. Give them all the water they require and feed them with a proprietary tomato feed once the first fruits are about the size of a pea. Maintain a moist atmosphere in the greenhouse to discourage red spider mite.

1 Choose a good-quality seed or multipurpose potting mixture and fill as many pots as you will need. Firm and level the surface of the soil.

2 Sow the seeds by spacing them out in a pot or small seed tray. This ensures that seedlings have plenty of room to stop them becoming lanky.

3 Space sowing also makes pricking out easier, as seedling roots do not become jumbled up and need not be pulled apart, which will damage them.

4 Sift some more of the same potting mix and cover the seeds to about their own depth. Never use too fine a sieve as the mix has a tendency to compact and retard germination. Water well.

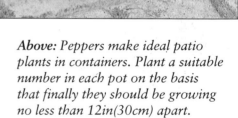

5 A stocky young plant, with the first two fruits growing well. If side shoots are reluctant to form, pinch out the tips of the main shoots to encourage them to develop.

Above: *Peppers make ideal patio plants in containers. Plant a suitable number in each pot on the basis that finally they should be growing no less than 12in(30cm) apart.*

Left: *Peppers come in all shapes and sizes and several colors. These large-fruited ones are ideal for cooking stuffed or just for slicing up as part of a summer salad.*

Eggplants (aubergines)

You can raise eggplants (aubergines) in exactly the same way as peppers, but as they require more heat than capsicums, it is better to leave the sowing until early to mid-spring or be prepared to keep them warmer. Do not overdo the heat, though, or they will become drawn, weak and useless. Aim at a temperature in the 60s°F (15-20°C). Never be tempted to take too many fruits from a plant or the size will suffer; four is ample. 'Moneymaker' is a good variety to choose.

When grown in a greenhouse, aubergines are especially susceptible to attacks of red spider mite. Although the plants are fairly well able to stand up for themselves, the mite will spread to other species with disastrous results. There is no reliable chemical control for the microscopic mites, but the predatory mite *Phytoseiulus* produces excellent results if you introduce it as soon as the leaves start to become speckled in the summer. This form of biological control is becoming widely available. In addition to this, you should keep the atmosphere in the greenhouse moist and reasonably cool, which in itself discourages the mite. Whitefly can also be a nuisance but they seldom reach the plague proportions they do with tomatoes. Yellow sticky traps hung above the plants will usually keep them under control, but if they fail, the parasitic *Encarsia* wasp will do the trick.

1 *Sow eggplant seeds singly in small pots For best results, plant them out into a growing bag in a greenhouse or sunroom when they have made a good root system.*

2 *Three plants in a standard-sized growing bag is ample, as they will grow to make large plants. Space the plants out evenly in the bag.*

3 *The top of the rootball should be just below the soil. Firming in the plants excludes air pockets and ensures that water is readily absorbed.*

4 Water thoroughly with at least a gallon (4 liters) of water. This should be all that is needed for 10-14 days. Do not feed at this stage.

5 When the stem is 6-8in(15-20cm) tall, nip out the top to encourage a good number of side shoots to form. It also prevents the plant getting too tall.

6 Nipping out also increases the crop by encouraging more flowers. Support the plants with canes once the weight of fruit bends the branches.

7 These plants have been 'stopped', the side shoots are growing away vigorously and the first flowers are beginning to show.

Once the first fruits are ready for cutting, it is unlikely any new flowers that form will have time to develop fruits.

8 Sooner than you realize, the shiny purple fruits start to form. Although normally needing greenhouse conditions in temperate climates, in a good summer eggplants will succeed outdoors in a sunny, sheltered spot.

Part Two

GROWING FRUIT

In the past, growing fruit in gardens was largely confined to bush and cane fruit, strawberries and, in larger gardens, the occasional apple tree. This was mainly because fruit trees were simply too large for most gardens. Today, however, with the introduction of dwarfing rootstocks and the consequent ability to grow far smaller fruit trees than before, there is no reason at all why you should not grow more or less any fruit that will flourish in the prevailing climate and that takes your fancy. In addition to this, it is easier than ever before to grow good crops of many of the most commonly grown fruits. The main reason for this is that breeding fruit in the last 40 or 50 years has been directed, in part, at creating new varieties that not only crop more heavily and earlier, but that are also more reliable and less susceptible to pests and diseases.

You might say that this has been paid for by a slight deterioration in some characteristics, such as flavor, but this is not as widespread as some like to imagine. The argument that 'you can't beat the old ones' can now be answered with 'oh yes you can', especially when it comes to cropping and reliability. Another thing that encourages some people to grow their own fruit applies equally to vegetables. It is the knowledge that they have only been sprayed with whatever you yourself have applied. All in all, there has never been a better time to start growing your own fruit, or for trying new and perhaps more exotic crops.

Left: Redcurrants sparkling in the sun. Right: A harvest of modern apples.

Planting and staking a young apple tree

The first thing to remember about planting an apple tree, or any other fruit tree, is that it should be with you for 20 years or more. This is a long time and you must make sure that the site and soil are absolutely right for it before you start. Any mistakes or omissions now will show themselves in future years. The site for all fruit trees must be sheltered from the wind and yet open to the sun. This is because pollinating insects will only work during the blossom period if the site is warm and free from wind.

Later in the year sunshine will ensure that the fruit develops its full flavor, and shelter from the wind will enable it to remain on the trees until it is ready for picking. Having chosen the right place for the tree, you must prepare the soil. Allow about 1sq.yd (1sq.m) for each tree. Dig the area and fork the base of the hole to improve the drainage and allow the roots to penetrate deeply. You must also dig in a good quantity of garden compost or manure to make the soil even better. Some recommendations are to add bonemeal to the ground after it has been dug. This is fine if you are planting in the fall or winter but in early spring it is far better to use a general fertilizer Bonemeal only helps new roots to form; a general feed will nourish the whole tree, including the new roots.

2 *Dig a hole large enough to take the root system and lay a cane across the top to show how deep to plant. the tree. Drive in a stake before planting so that you do not damage the roots later on.*

3 *Replace some of the soil in the hole and gently rock the tree about to shake the soil down amongst the roots. Tread it down firmly.*

Using a tree tie

1 *Nail the buckle end of the tree tie to the stake, pass the free end round the tree and bring it back through the plastic ring.*

4 To shape a normal 'bush' tree, select and retain four or five suitable shoots as the future main branches. Start by shortening them by one third to half their length.

Most of the retained shoots are set at a fairly wide angle to the main stem. This gives strong joints that are most unlikely to break under heavy crops.

5 The result of these early stages of pruning is a well-shaped and balanced tree that will produce a strong framework of branches able to carry good crops of healthy apples.

6 By midsummer, the young tree has produced many more shoots. Leave them until the winter, when you can carry out the appropriate pruning to encourage more branches to form.

Only cut out those branches that are rubbing or causing overcrowding. Harmless ones can be left to fruit.

Left: The same principles apply to planting a tree growing in a container, but remember to remove the bag and any other packaging before you start.

2 Push the end of the tie through the buckle so that the tree is held firmly but not too tightly, and away from the stake.

3 Push the tie back through the plastic ring to stop it slipping. If plastic ties are stiff, dip them in warm water.

Cordons and espaliers

The cordon is the simplest way of training apple and pear trees intensively. Once you have the principle under control, you can create many interesting and fruitful shapes. Cordons are best planted and trained at a 45° angle to reduce their vigor and encourage fruiting. Cut back any side shoots that are present at planting to three buds straight afterwards. When side shoots appear in subsequent years, prune them in the same way but in late summer. After that, when shoots grow from those already pruned back, shorten the new ones in late summer back to just one bud. Summer pruning encourages fruit buds and fruiting spurs to form. The espalier is really just a vertical cordon but with pairs of horizontal branches 10-12in(25-30cm) apart. Espaliers are trained to wires and can be grown against a wall or in the open. You can form an espalier either by training out a tier of branches to their full length before going up to the next or by starting a fresh tier every year and developing them all together. To grow a tier a year, start with a single-stemmed tree with no side shoots and cut it back to a bud just above and pointing out from the bottom wire. The next two buds down will form the first tier of horizontal branches and the top bud will extend the stem upwards. From then on, do the same every winter until the tree is as tall as you want.

Columnar trees

The new compact columnar (Ballerina) trees, have very close leaves and buds and an almost complete absence of side shoots. They are ideally suited to growing in pots and make first-rate patio trees. Because of their growth habit they require hardly any pruning.

1 Cordon and espalier apples and pears are best pruned at this stage; in the late summer when they have stopped growing. Winter pruning has less advantages, but will cause no harm.

Reducing the complexity of the spur improves sap flow to the developing fruitlets.

2 This spur has already reached a reasonable size. Do not allow it to grow any larger, so cut back the extension growth to a fruit bud. This will increase the fruit size.

3 Whether done in late summer or winter, pruning is the same. Cut back new shoots growing from main stems to 3in(7.5cm), and those from previously pruned spurs to 1in(2.5cm).

Above: *The step-over, or horizontal, cordon is another attractive and space-saving way of growing apples. Grow them beside a path to make them easy to tend.*

Above: *The same tree in full summer growth with a useful crop of apples. It is ready for summer pruning to improve the fruits' size and color. This also reduces pests and diseases.*

Family trees

You can buy fruit trees made up of more than one variety of the same fruit. This family apple tree is in full flower and clearly shows the three varieties grafted onto the same rootstock. Ideally, they should all flower together for good pollination, but an overlap of a few days is enough.

'Discovery' - reliable, early dessert apple.

4 *By midsummer the criss-cross cordon is growing well and carrying a promising crop. Any fruit thinning must wait until the natural 'drop' is over.*

'Fiesta' - a new, late-keeping, Coxlike variety with an excellent flavor.

'Sunset' - prolific midseason with small fruit.

Pears

Pears are as easy to grow as apples and choice varieties are absolutely delicious. They can be grown in the same tree shapes and sizes as apples, but are even better for growing as cordons and espaliers, because they form fruit buds more readily. You can turn this virtue to your advantage by growing the small, free-standing (not trained) trees called 'dwarf pyramids', which are conical in shape and carry heavy crops. They take up little room and are a good shape for growing in pots and tubs. In management they come between cordons and normal trees. Pears are slightly less easy to assess for ripeness than apples and tend to deteriorate more quickly once they are ripe, so pick pears and ripen them indoors.

Although the choicer varieties are traditionally French and require plenty of summer sun to give of their best, there are some extremely good varieties that succeed well in the cooler summers. A better dessert variety than 'Williams', but slightly later, is 'Onward'. It inherits its juiciness and excellent flavor from 'Comice', one of its parents. 'Comice' ripens later, in mid- to late fall, and is certainly a supreme dessert variety, but it takes a lot of growing to get the best from it. A more reliable alternative is the new 'Concorde'. It ripens at about the same time as 'Conference' and is a 'Comice'/'Conference' cross. The best cooking pear is 'Catillac'.

Above: The espalier, which originated in France, is a series of horizontal cordons growing from a central stem. Again, summer pruning is advisable.

Right: Oblique cordons are one of the most economical ways of growing pears. Most varieties readily form fruiting spurs .

Left: For many years 'Conference' has been a popular garden and commercial pear. It combines good cropping with an acceptable flavor. The cropping is encouraged by its high fertility.

Right: 'Comice' (full name 'Doyenne du Comice') is probably the best flavored pear there is. However, it can be a shy cropper and needs at the very least one other variety, and preferably more, planted nearby to ensure good cross-pollination.

Below: Although not widely grown in Europe, 'Clapp's Favorite' is a good-quality American, late-summer pear. It is sweet and juicy, if slightly sharp. Eat when it is ready; it soon goes over.

Right: 'Concorde' is a cross between probably the best flavored pear, 'Comice', and the most reliable one, 'Conference'. It has the heavy cropping of 'Conference' and a much improved flavor through 'Comice'. It ripens in early fall.

Left: *A messy hole on the surface of the fruit signifies codling moth caterpillar attack. Damage is visible from early summer onwards, but at this stage control is impossible.*

Cut open a damaged apple and the core area will be black and revolting. You may find the offending pink maggot.

Setting a trap to catch the codling moth

One of the most troublesome pests of apples - and to a lesser extent of pears - is the codling moth. It is the caterpillar of this moth that you often find as a maggot in home-grown apples. The adult moth is a little larger than a clothes moth and lays its eggs on the surface of the fruitlets in late spring and early summer. It is essential that you destroy the caterpillars that hatch from these eggs before they have time to eat into the fruit. You can do this by spraying with, for example, a permethrin insecticide in early summer and again two weeks later. However, a much more convenient and non-chemical method involves attracting and trapping the male moths on a sort of flypaper. This greatly reduces the number of fertile eggs laid and, hence, the number of caterpillars that hatch out. If a trap catches more than about five moths a night or, say, fifteen in a week, then you should spray as well, because you will never catch all the moths. If you catch very few moths, then trapping may be the only control needed. Many garden centers now sell codling moth traps or you can buy them by mail order from a number of sources. There is also a trap available for the red plum maggot (plum fruit moth), an equally serious pest. Both traps are 100% specific and will only catch the one kind of moth.

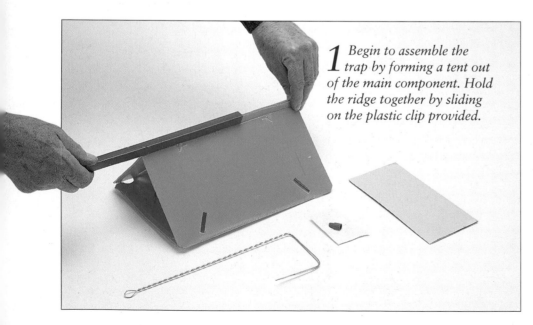

1 *Begin to assemble the trap by forming a tent out of the main component. Hold the ridge together by sliding on the plastic clip provided.*

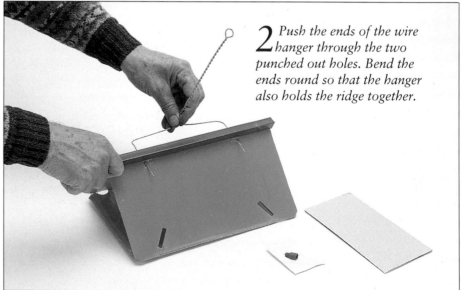

2 *Push the ends of the wire hanger through the two punched out holes. Bend the ends round so that the hanger also holds the ridge together.*

3 *The 'flypaper' is folded with the sticky surface inside. Peel the card apart carefully so that the glue stays on the card.*

4 *A piece of rubber impregnated with the female pheromone (scent attractant) is the bait. Place it in the center of the sticky card.*

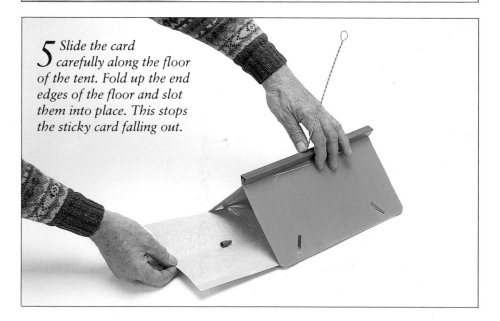

5 *Slide the card carefully along the floor of the tent. Fold up the end edges of the floor and slot them into place. This stops the sticky card falling out.*

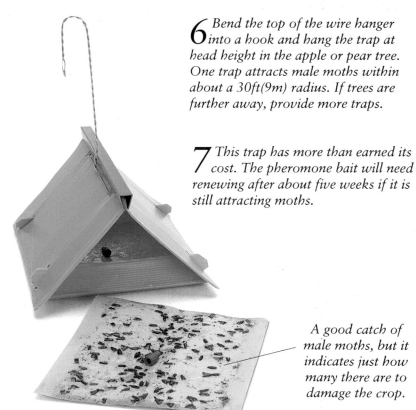

6 *Bend the top of the wire hanger into a hook and hang the trap at head height in the apple or pear tree. One trap attracts male moths within about a 30ft(9m) radius. If trees are further away, provide more traps.*

7 *This trap has more than earned its cost. The pheromone bait will need renewing after about five weeks if it is still attracting moths.*

A good catch of male moths, but it indicates just how many there are to damage the crop.

73

Storing fruit

Only apples and pears can be stored as they are; all other fruits must first be prepared and then frozen, bottled, etc. Late-ripening dessert apples and cooking apples destined for storing can be picked all at once. Pick dessert pears when they are still hard and allow them to ripen indoors. Cooking pears are picked and cooked or stored when hard. When dessert pears are ready for picking, they part quite readily from the tree.

When picking any fruit, but particularly if it is to be stored, treat it gently, as any damage before, during or after picking will ruin it for storage. Only store fruit that is completely sound. For the longest storage, keep apples and pears just a few degrees above freezing. Choose a suitable brick shed or garage and make sure that it contains no material that is likely to taint the fruit. Look at the fruit regularly and remove any that are bad or ready to eat. Apples can be either wrapped and boxed, put in cell-pack boxes or laid out on shelves or racks. Always put pears on racks, as they need air.

1 A good way of keeping apples is in boxes of cell-packs that you will often find being thrown out by shops and other fruit retailers.

2 Place one apple in each cell of the 'concertina'. This keeps them apart, so that any rot will not pass from one fruit to the next.

3 Put a dividing sheet of paper in between each layer of fruit. This not only helps to keep the fruits apart, but also makes the pack more stable.

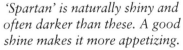

4 Carry on filling the box with fruit until it is full. Always keep just one variety in a box; different varieties seldom ripen at the same time.

The amount of russet is immaterial, but the green ground color shows that this 'Conference' pear is not yet ripe.

This fruit is ready for eating. The green has turned yellow and the flesh will give when pressed.

Apples are best left with the natural bloom on when stored and certainly on the show bench.

'Spartan' is naturally shiny and often darker than these. A good shine makes it more appetizing.

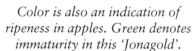

Left: *Another good way of storing apples is to wrap them individually in kitchen paper. As with cell-packed fruits, this prevents the spread of any storage rot that may appear after a while.*

Below: *Storing apples and pears on racks is possibly the best way, but also takes up the most room. Air can circulate, and ripe or rotting fruit is easy to see.*

5 *Once the box is full, lay a piece of card or a folded newspaper on top and put it away in a cool, dark and airy place to store the apples.*

Above: *This is a homemade model that has the added advantage of being mouse-proof by virtue of the wire netting back and front.*

Color is also an indication of ripeness in apples. Green denotes immaturity in this 'Jonagold'.

Once the ground color changes to yellow, bring the fruit into a warm room to finish ripening.

Exactly the same ripeness indications are seen in a wholly green variety when unripe.

When ripe, this 'Crispin' mellows to yellow, with a blush on the cheek.

Planting a peach tree or nectarine

Essentially, you grow and treat peaches and nectarines in exactly the same way; the nectarine was originally a hairless 'sport' found growing on a peach tree. Even today, you occasionally find nectarines on peach trees and vice versa. Everything, therefore, that is said about growing peaches refers equally to nectarines. They come from the Mediterranean and, as such, are not completely at home or hardy in cooler climates, so give them the warmest position available in the garden. They also flower early in spring and you will normally need to hand pollinate them because few pollinating insects have emerged from hibernation when the blossom is out. Hand pollination of the flowers is very easy. Wait for a warm, sunny day when the flowers are open. Using an artist's soft paintbrush or even a piece of absorbent cotton, draw it over the open flower. This collects pollen from the anthers and transfers some to the receptive stigma. Given relatively warm weather, fertilization will follow and a fruit will develop. If there is a good set of fruit you will probably need to thin the fruitlets to ensure that fruit size does not suffer. Carry out a first thinning in early summer when the fruitlets are the size of a hazelnut, so that they are 4in(10cm) apart. Follow this with a second thinning two to three weeks later, when they have reached walnut size. Aim to leave the fruitlets about 8in(20cm) apart. Reliable varieties of peach for outdoors include 'Peregrine' and 'Rochester'. 'Early Rivers' and 'Lord Napier' are good nectarines.

1 *A young peach tree straight from the garden center. When planting it, use the rootball to judge the size of hole you need to dig.*

2 *Once firmly planted, the tree should be very slightly deeper than it was in its original pot, so that new roots form from the stock.*

3 *Now comes the hard part. Cut back the tree to leave two suitable shoots to form the first rays of the fan. This treatment means that you can start training from the right basis.*

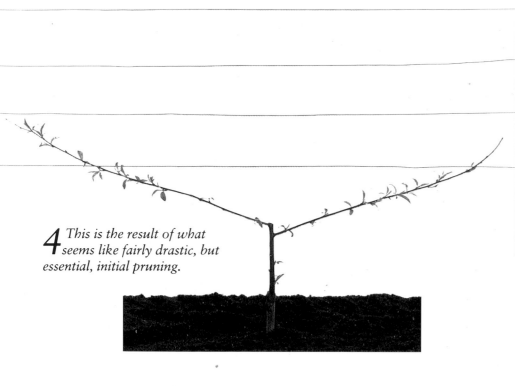

4 This is the result of what seems like fairly drastic, but essential, initial pruning.

5 Cut back these two shoots to two-thirds to threequarters of their original length. Prune to a bud on the upper surface of the shoot so that the resulting growth grows upwards.

6 Tie two primary training canes to permanent wires, 9-12in(23-30cm) apart. Use plastic string, as it lasts longer. Wire is even better, but bend the sharp ends out of harm's way.

7 This is how the tree and canes will look when they are all in position. The ends of the canes are close to the tree.

8 Using soft string, tie the shoots to the canes, but not too tightly. This avoids strangling the shoots as they grow, which can happen with plastic.

9 The tree is on the point of starting to send out new shoots from the two that were trained in. If necessary, protect the tender growths from frost.

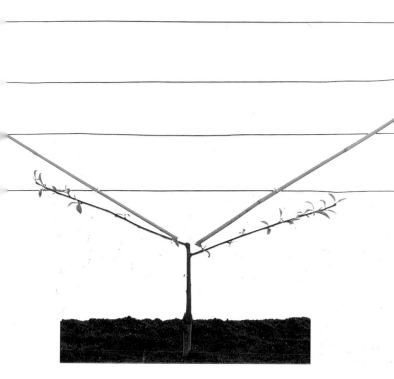

Tying the shoots to a cane helps them to grow straight and lends support when they bear fruit.

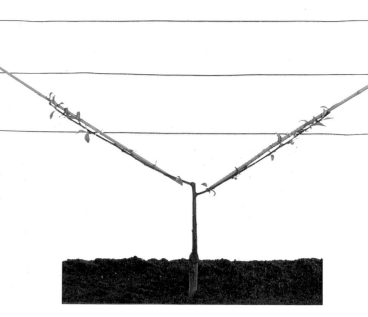

Training a peach tree

Being natives of the Mediterranean, peaches and nectarines can seldom be grown as free-standing trees in the open garden in cooler countries. To give of their best they should be fan-trained against a warm, sunny wall or fence. Given the choice, a wall is better than a fence because the brickwork holds a great deal more heat. This is released at night and will frequently raise the temperature around the tree sufficiently to keep away a slight frost. The sequence of training a tree in a fan shape started on page 76 continues here. Try to follow the guidelines as closely as possible because what is done in the early years has a big influence on the tree's future.

Unquestionably, the worst affliction to attack a peach or nectarine tree is a disfiguring fungus disease called peach leaf curl. This causes first the young leaves and then the older ones to become blistered, swollen and bright red. Control is difficult, but covering the fan-trained trees with plastic when it rains during the growing season keeps the leaves dry and greatly reduces the spread of this devastating fungus. Another approach is to make two applications of a copper spray, a week apart, at leaf-fall and another two when the buds have started to grow out in spring. These will go a long way to control the fungus.

1 *By midsummer the tree is growing well. The right side is more vigorous than the left; correct this later by appropriate pruning.*

2 *Fix another cane in position for a new shoot. Tie it temporarily to the stem of the tree to help training and release it at a later stage.*

3 *Tie the shoot that has developed from the lower surface of the main branch to the new cane. This will become the lowest branch.*

4 *Fix another cane for the shoot growing from the upper surface of the branch. Pinch off any shoots that are pointing away from the tree.*

5 *As before, tie in all the new shoots with soft string, but do so quite loosely to avoid any constriction of the shoot. Examine all ties regularly.*

Above: *The reward for attentive management; a crop of delicious peaches in the making.*

The bareness on this side of the tree can be overcome by appropriate pruning and by tying the weak branch into a more upright position until it grows more strongly.

6 *Although it is still summer, the tree has almost finished its first growing season. There will be little further growth from now on.*

Plums, gages and damsons

Plums of all sorts are becoming more popular these days. The smaller trees grown on the rootstock 'Pixy' are much easier to manage, and you can grow plum trees as cordons and fans trained against walls and fences, 'festooned' trees with their branches tied down to encourage fruiting and also pyramid trees. Spring frosts are still a problem, but with the smaller, more compact trees simply drape some horticultural fleece over them on spring evenings when a frost is likely to strike. However, you should still grow plums in a sheltered and sunny part of the garden because this helps the fruit to ripen. In its early years, concentrate on forming the tree and building up its branches by appropriate pruning. Later, though, ordinary bush trees require very little attention beyond the removal of shoots and branches that are dead or diseased, crossing or crowding, or that are growing too high, too low or are too spreading.

There are very few plum diseases to bother you. The worst is the silver leaf fungus in which the normal green of the leaves develops a metallic sheen. The best way of preventing this is to prune when the tree is in leaf, because the fungus only spreads in the winter and by entering fresh wounds. The red plum maggot is also tiresome, but it can now be controlled with a specific pheromone trap, similar to the codling moth (see pages 72-73). 'Victoria' is still the most reliable variety for gardens. A good early cooker is 'Czar', while 'Kirke's Blue' and 'Cambridge Gage' are better eaters than 'Victoria'. The 'Prune' or 'Shropshire' damson has the best flavor but 'Farleigh' the heaviest crops.

1 This tree has already been trained in the nursery as a fan. Four branches are all that are needed so the rest are removed with clean secateurs.

2 Cut close to the topmost shoot that is to be retained so that the wound will quickly heal over and exclude any harmful fungal rots.

Left: Although not often seen in gardens, 'Marjorie's Seedling' is a reliable cooker. The tree is tall but flowers and fruits late, so is useful in frosty areas.

Below: Damsons are small cooking plums that often crop prolifically. 'Bradley's King' crops in early fall. One of the largest and best-flavored damsons.

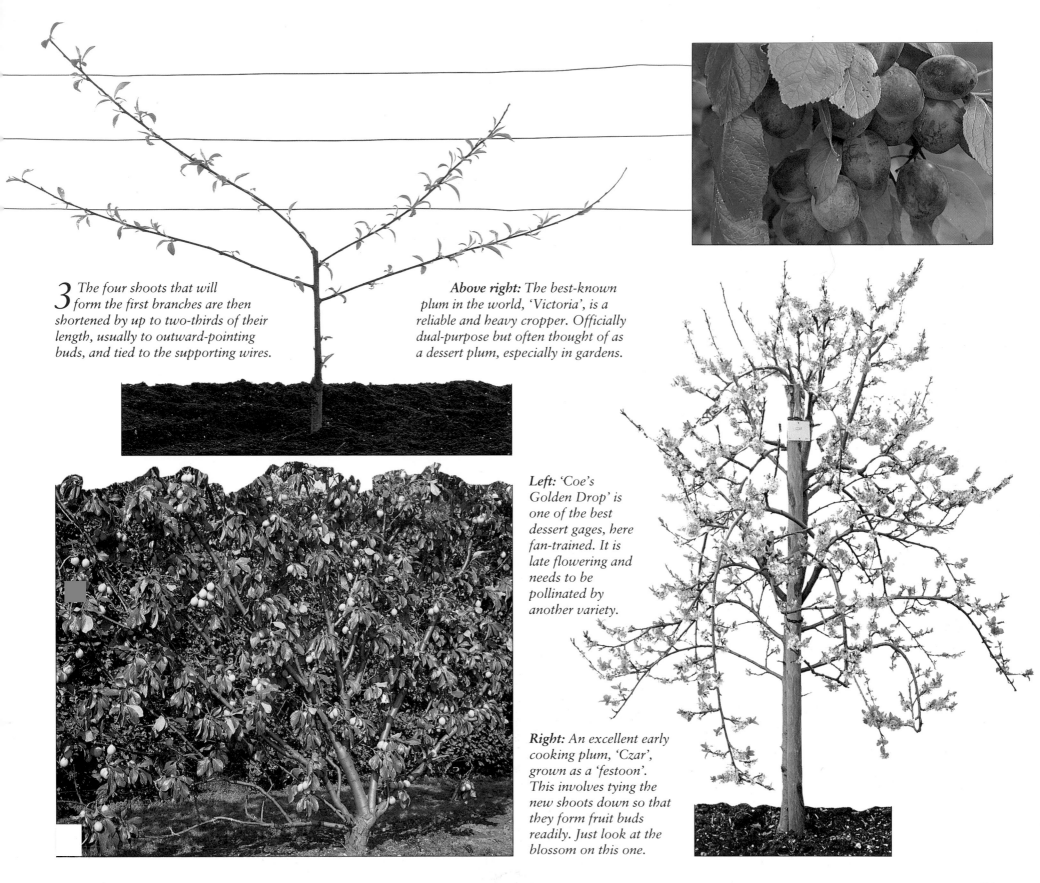

3 The four shoots that will form the first branches are then shortened by up to two-thirds of their length, usually to outward-pointing buds, and tied to the supporting wires.

Above right: The best-known plum in the world, 'Victoria', is a reliable and heavy cropper. Officially dual-purpose but often thought of as a dessert plum, especially in gardens.

Left: 'Coe's Golden Drop' is one of the best dessert gages, here fan-trained. It is late flowering and needs to be pollinated by another variety.

Right: An excellent early cooking plum, 'Czar', grown as a 'festoon'. This involves tying the new shoots down so that they form fruit buds readily. Just look at the blossom on this one.

*1 Before planting a young
gooseberry bush such as this,
remove any shoots that are closer
than about 5in(13cm) to the roots,
as well as any buds among the roots.*

Growing gooseberries

Gooseberries need good soil conditions to give of their best. This is especially true of dessert varieties, which are grown to a larger size than cookers. Take care when tending bushes or picking fruit, as the thorns are long, pointed and very sharp. One of the best ways of growing gooseberries is as cordons trained to a wall or fence or grow them in the open up canes. They are much easier to look after than bushes, the dessert varieties ripen better and you are less likely to be scratched. You can grow cordons with just one vertical shoot, or double or multiple cordons with two or more shoots. Single cordons are the quickest to reach the desired height but you need many more plants for a given length of fence. Another unusual shape is the standard, which, like a standard rose, is just a bush on top of a 3-4ft(90-120cm) stem. Ordinary bushes take up rather a lot of room and are not as easy to maintain. 'Careless' or 'Jubilee Careless' are the most prolific cookers, with 'Leveller' an excellent all-round dessert variety.

2 Plant the bush firmly, leaving a clear leg of 5-6in(13-15cm) between the ground and the first branch. Nick out any buds on the leg.

3 After planting, prune the bush by removing any weak shoots, cutting back misplaced ones and shortening the rest by roughly half their length.

Taking gooseberry cuttings

Gooseberries are easy to propagate. Simply take hardwood cuttings, retaining just the top three or four buds, and insert them into V-slits in the ground 6in(15cm) apart. Push the cuttings into the ground as near upright as possible so that the resulting bushes have a vertical 'leg'. The best time to take cuttings is in early winter as soon as the leaves have fallen.

Left: 'Whitesmith' is a first-rate dessert gooseberry. It crops well and has an excellent flavor. The medium vigor of the bush makes it very suitable for growing as a cordon.

Below: A row of well-trained and maintained 'U' cordons cropping well after three or four years growth. Net the fruit to protect it from birds.

4 Pruning stimulates side shoots, so that the original four or five 'branches' give rise to eight to ten after the first growing season. This forms the framework of the bush.

5 For a U-cordon (with two upright stems), prune back the bush to two strong shoots growing out opposite each other.

Bend the two shoots down carefully and tie them as horizontally as possible.

Pruning gooseberries

For the biggest and best dessert gooseberries, prune both cordons and bushes in early summer. That is also the time to thin out the fruits to one per cluster, using the thinnings for cooking. Summer pruning simply involves cutting back the new shoots (those you do not want for extension growth) to five leaves, about 5in(13cm). Summer pruning improves the berry size and color of dessert varieties and the crop weight of cookers. Early to midsummer is the normal and the most beneficial time to summer prune. Because you are removing the soft growth at the end of the shoots, which is the part most susceptible to attack by mildew, summer pruning also plays a very valuable role in controlling this disease. As well as this, you should also spray with benomyl or carbendazim. As far as pests are concerned, the gooseberry sawfly is the worst. Control it by spraying with permethrin or derris in mid-spring. Unfortunately, there are no thornless varieties worth growing, but cordons are a great deal less painful to look after than normal bushes.

1 A mature, unpruned gooseberry bush in winter has shoots and branches growing in all directions and everything is covered in thorns.

2 Remove all shoots and branches growing too low or too far out. Crossing branches and those crowding others must also go.

3 Once the framework is tamed and tidied up, begin shortening all the branch leaders (young shoots on the end of each branch) to half their length.

This is a strong, young branch that will carry heavy crops.

Below: 'Early Sulphur' ripens early, is a heavy cropper and makes an upright bush. Do not be put off by the bristles on the fruits; a superb dessert variety.

Right: 'Lancashire Lad' is a large-berried, coarsely bristled but popular dessert variety. It ripens in early to midseason and has a good flavor.

Above: 'Leveller' is a heavy cropper, with good flavor that ripens mid- to late season. The main commercial dessert variety.

4 Shorten side shoots on existing spurs or growing straight from main branches to 3in(7.5cm) to an up- or outward-pointing bud.

Completely remove any weak shoots.

5 The tidily pruned bush is well equipped to carry heavy crops without collapsing under the strain. Upright training counteracts the gooseberry's natural weeping habit.

1 *Make sure that you start with a good-quality, strong growing bush. This one-year-old example has three vigorous shoots and a good root system.*

Blackcurrants are an excellent soft fruit for making into jellies and fruit fools, for filling pies and fruit tarts and they make a novel addition to summer fruit salads. They are also exceptionally rich in vitamin C and can be used for cordial or wine-making. Unfortunately, traditional bushes of most varieties are too large for many gardens, but by choosing a more compact variety and pruning it harder than normal, they become a more viable proposition. Nor is it possible to grow blackcurrants as cordons, because their best fruits and heaviest crops are produced on young shoots, which are removed when pruning cordons. Blackcurrants are very easy to propagate using hardwood cuttings taken in the early winter. You can start as soon as the leaves drop in late fall.

The worst pest is the blackcurrant gall mite. Not only does it cause the buds to become swollen and stay closed in spring, but it also spreads the virus disease reversion. There is no cure for either condition, so be sure to pull up and burn any bushes bearing even just a few of the unopened, pea-sized buds in spring. Both the mites and reversion are confined to blackcurrants.

2 *Dig out a hole wide enough to take the root system and deep enough to allow the bush to be planted about 2in(5cm) deeper than it was before.*

Spread out the roots in the planting hole.

4 *After planting at the correct depth (shown here) completely remove all the weak shoots and shorten the remainder to two or three buds long.*

3 *Cover with soil. Shake the bush so that each root is in contact with the earth. Firm down soil to prevent it drying out and to support the bush.*

Taking cuttings

1 *Push a spade into the ground 8-9in(20-23cm) deep and lever back on the handle to form a slit to receive the prepared cuttings.*

2 *Prepare cuttings in midwinter from strong, straight, healthy one-year-old shoots. Carefully cut back thin tips to a strong bud.*

3 *Cut the base of the shoot to a strong bud. The cutting should be straight and strong and 9-12in(23-30cm) long.*

7 *Here is the same bush the following summer. There are at least three new strong shoots. These will not be pruned and will start fruiting the following summer.*

4 *Push cuttings into the slit 6in (15cm) apart, so that only the top buds are visible. Strong shoots will come from below ground.*

5 *Push the soil down around the cuttings really well so that they are firmly in place for the winter. There is no need to water them in.*

Generally speaking, you should prune back to an outward-pointing bud.

5 *This harsh treatment encourages strong shoots to grow from the base and stimulates the root system, so that the bush establishes quickly.*

6 *Always cut back to a bud that in the following growing season will give rise to a new shoot developing in the desired direction.*

6 *These cuttings have two buds showing above the surface, but do not worry if there is only one.*

Pruning blackcurrants

The aim of pruning is to keep the bushes young and as compact as possible. It helps to choose the least vigorous variety, the relatively new 'Ben Sarek', with a recommended planting distance of 36in(90cm), instead of the more normal 48in(1.2m). Blackcurrants are usually pruned in early winter by cutting out branch systems when they reach four years old. If you want to keep the bushes small, reduce this to three or even two years. Because the bushes will be smaller, also reduce the planting distance between them in the first place or the crop from a given length of row will be considerably lighter. A simple way to establish the age of a branch is to start with the young shoot at the tip and count backwards down the branch. Each year's growth is darker. As well as 'Ben Sarek', other good garden varieties include 'Ben Lomond' and 'Ben Connan'.
This is a new one that is reputed to have the largest individual currants of all and to have good disease-resistance, too.

Right: Jostaberry, a vigorous hybrid between blackcurrant and gooseberry, crops heavily and may be trained and pruned into many shapes and sizes.

1 Even a well-tended blackcurrant bush can seem daunting when you come to prune it. In fact, you need only follow a few simple rules.

2 Cut out all branches growing too close to the ground, across the bush or that are more than three years old. Eliminate any that cause congestion.

5 A two-year-old branch. The central stem fruited in the previous summer and produced the side shoots that will fruit next year. Then you may need to remove it.

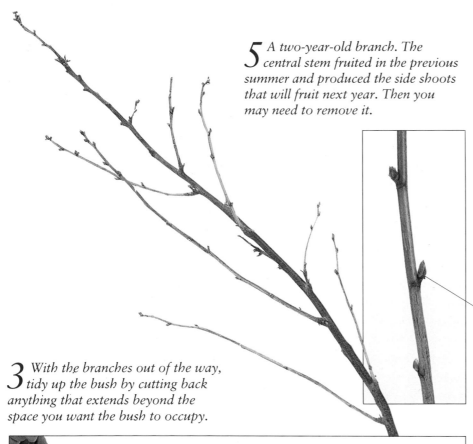

Right: *'Ben Sarek' is a relative newcomer among blackcurrants. The bush is significantly smaller than other varieties, yet it is heavy cropping. An excellent garden variety.*

A one-year-old blackcurrant shoot. Note the fat fruit buds that will carry fruit next summer. Do not remove a shoot like this.

3 With the branches out of the way, tidy up the bush by cutting back anything that extends beyond the space you want the bush to occupy.

4 Virtually no shoots have been shortened. If one is too long, cut it right out. Shortening a young shoot encourages growth and branching, which makes it even larger.

Redcurrants and whitecurrants

This shoot arises too close to the base of the stem and needs cutting out straight away.

Cultivated not as conventional bushes but as cordons, both redcurrants, and their colorless cousins the whitecurrants, take up very little room and will grow either in the open garden trained to canes or against a wall or fence. U-cordons are more economical of plants than single vertical cordons, but the latter will cover the area more quickly. Pruning is best carried out in early summer by cutting back the new shoots to within 4in(10cm) of the main branches and, further, to 2in(5cm) in the winter. Summer pruning encourages the currants to grow and ripen and also reduces the amount of soft, sappy growth, which would be susceptible to mildew disease. The Dutch variety 'Jonkheer van Tets' (early) and 'Red Lake' (midseason) are both excellent in gardens. Grow 'Stanza' for a late crop. 'White Versailles' is the most widely grown whitecurrant. Propagate both kinds by hardwood cuttings in early winter. Although mildew is sometimes seen, it is never as serious as it is on gooseberries. The worst pests are usually aphids that cause red blisters to form on leaves. If this is serious, any systemic insecticide will control them.

This young and well positioned shoot will make a fruitful branch.

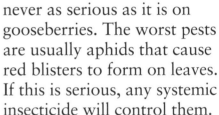

Shorten strong shoots to an outwardly pointing bud.

2 *For the same reason, nick out any buds that you see among the roots. If left in place, they would produce unwanted suckers later on.*

1 *Start with a strong, one-year-old bush. As it is best grown on a short 'leg', remove any shoots that are less than about 5in(13cm) from the roots.*

3 *Make the planting hole wide enough to take the spread-out root system and deep enough to leave the planted bush just deeper than before.*

4 *After planting, remove weak shoots. Cut back strong but badly placed shoots to 1in(2.5cm). Shorten remaining shoots by half their length.*

2 *Shorten the branch leaders (the year-old top section) by half and cut back unwanted side shoots to about 2in(5cm).*

A cluster of fruit buds. Pruning will encourage more buds to form. Do not cut these buds off.

Taking cuttings

Propagating redcurrants and whitecurrants is largely the same as for blackcurrants (page 87). Only retain the top four buds, however, and push in the cutting to leave 6in(15cm) between the lowest retained bud and the ground. Insert 6in(15cm) apart.

1 *To prune an established bush, remove any low, broken or crossing branches, plus any that are clearly causing overcrowding.*

Left: White-currants are more of a novelty. The crops are not as heavy, but the flavor is similar to redcurrants. They require the same cultivation.

Left: 'Jonkheer van Tets' is a heavy-cropping redcurrant, very early and of high quality. It is widely available.

Right: The pink currant makes an interesting addition to a fruit garden, and has the same qualities as the reds.

Planting strawberries

1 Buy strong, bare-rooted plants in late summer or early fall. This one was propagated just a few weeks previously. Do not be tempted to choose larger but older plants growing in pots.

2 Use a garden line to mark the row and make a hole deep enough to take the whole root system without having to bend the roots to fit them in.

3 It is important that the base of the leaves are at soil level. If the tops of the roots are visible, they are not planted deep enough.

Strawberries are probably the most popular and easily grown fruit, and you can include some plants even in the smallest garden. As well as the traditional rows of plants in the vegetable section, you can also grow strawberries in pots, tower pots, growing-bags, hanging baskets, windowboxes and other planters or even as edging plants in the flower garden. You can use the fruits in many ways, to make desserts, jellies and in all sorts of puddings. They are truly a versatile and delicious fruit.

Strawberry varieties are either of the summer-fruiting or perpetual-fruiting type. Summer-fruiting are the most popular and you can advance them under cloches or even in an unheated greenhouse. For later crops, use one of the perpetual varieties. These will start flowering and fruiting naturally at about the same time as the summer ones, but by removing the flowers as they appear until very early summer, you can induce them to fruit from late summer often until late fall, depending on the weather.

The worst disease is unquestionably botrytis (gray mold), which turns the fruits into gray puffballs of fungus. You can reduce the infection by putting down straw between the rows or using a proprietary alternative to keep mud off the fruit. In addition, spray fortnightly with benomyl once the first flowers are showing color. Strawberries will nearly always need netting against birds. If you want to keep summer-fruiting varieties for another year, cut off the leaves, old fruit stalks and unwanted runners after fruiting. This cleans away many pests and diseases and rejuvenates the plants. This 'haircut' is not essential but it is certainly beneficial. If you give them a high-potash feed at the same time, they will build up into strong plants for the winter and following year.

Below: Delicious crops of strawberries like this are perfectly possible if you take care over them and grow modern varieties, such as 'Elsanta'.

1 Once the baby strawberries are about the size of a pea, you must cover the ground under the plants with straw or mats.

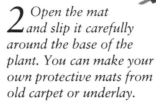

2 Open the mat and slip it carefully around the base of the plant. You can make your own protective mats from old carpet or underlay.

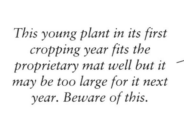

This young plant in its first cropping year fits the proprietary mat well but it may be too large for it next year. Beware of this.

Above: Netting to protect the crop is vital. This system is splendid; it saves the strawberries and looks attractive.

Left: Strawberries this large are often utterly tasteless. Not so 'Maxim'. However, this size of fruit is only found in the first crop. After that it returns to a more normal size.

3 Work plenty of clean straw well under the plants so that the fruitlets are not splashed with rain and mud, which usually leads to botrytis.

1 *Propagate strawberries from the plantlets that form at the end of 'runners'. These grow from the main plant in the summer.*

2 *Fill some pots with used potting mixture and sink them in the ground around the plant whose plantlets will be used for propagation.*

The number of runners and plantlets produced will vary with the variety. Never use more than five per plant or they are likely to be weak.

Propagating strawberries

Because new plantlets are naturally produced on 'runners' sent out by established plants, propagating from your own strawberries is so easy that it is sometimes done without a thought for the snags involved. The main - and very important one - is that you could be using plants that are infected with a virus disease. Clearly that is a recipe for disaster, as the new plants will also be infected and will never crop well. There is no doubt that if you are uncertain about the health of your plants, the only sensible action is to buy new ones that carry a health certificate from a nursery or garden center. However, assuming that all is well, the first thing to do is to select what you consider to be the best parent plants. They should be strong-growing, free from pests and diseases, and good croppers. Make the selection during the early part of the growing season and into the fruiting period, so that you can start propagating straight after the plants have fruited in early to midsummer. It is also a good idea to work out beforehand how many new plants you will need. On the basis of rooting no more than five plantlets per parent plant, you will then know how many plants you need to nominate as parent plants.

The simplest way to propagate strawberries is to peg down the plantlets (one per runner and leaving them attached) onto the soil surface near the parent. However, it can be inconvenient having the new plants dotted about all over the place, so a much better plan is to peg them into 7-9in(18-23cm) pots of old potting mixture. Not only is rooting quicker into the more friendly medium, but you can also move the rooted plants after they have been parted from the parent a month later.

3 *Leaving it attached to the parent plant, peg the plantlet down into the potting mixture with a piece of looped wire. This will prevent any movement during rooting.*

Below: Although you could use all three plantlets on this runner, it is better to choose just the strongest one.

This is the runner from the parent. The plantlet grew from the end of it.

6 Remove the remains of the runner and any dead leaves and flower stalks. If planted by early fall, you can expect a full crop the next summer.

4 The pot may be watered after 'layering' the plantlet to settle the potting mixture, but that is usually the only time any watering is needed.

5 After about a month, a good root system will have developed in the pot and you can cut the new plant from the parent.

7 Dig a hole large enough to hold the rootball comfortably. Make sure it is sufficiently deep to allow the base of the leaves to sit at soil level after planting.

8 Push the soil back around the rootball and firm it in well to exclude all the air pockets. This leads to quick rooting.

9 Water the plant in to settle it into its new planting position. It now has every chance of producing a heavy crop of fruit the following summer.

95

Raspberries

Raspberries are a popular and easy-to-grow soft fruit. The most convenient way to grow them is in rows in the vegetable garden, although by planting them in groups of three it is quite possible to grow just a few in mixed borders or elsewhere tied to stakes. There are two types of raspberry: summer-fruiting and fall-fruiting. Apart from the obvious difference, the main one is that the fall varieties produce canes that fruit later in the same season, whereas the canes of summer varieties grow during the first year and fruit in the summer of the second year.

Each cane carries just one crop of fruit and the pruning strategy is based on this. With summer varieties, cut down the fruited canes straight after fruiting and tie in the new ones to the wires in their place. All the canes of the fall varieties fruit together. Once they have fruited, leave them until new ones start to appear above ground in the following spring and then cut all the previous year's canes to the ground.

Left: Good, bare-root summer-fruiting raspberry canes are available during the late fall or in winter. Avoid containerized plants, as they are far more expensive and no better.

1 *Plant the canes 15in(38cm) apart, so that all the roots and any buds on them are below the surface. These buds will grow out to produce the following year's canes.*

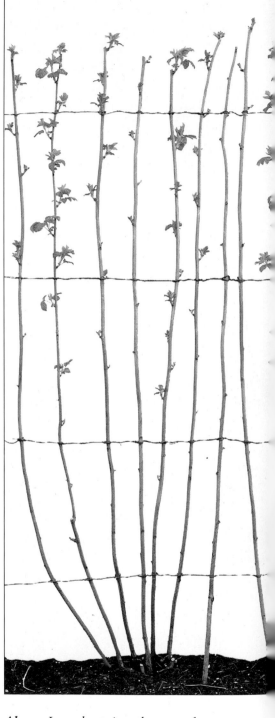

Above: In early spring, the canes from these well-established plants are starting to send out the side shoots that will carry the fruit. Notice the ample spacing and supporting wires.

2 *Immediately after planting, cut back the canes leaving them about 10in(25cm) long. This will allow just a few new shoots to grow from them in the following year.*

Some fruit will develop on the side shoots next year. Only allow a very few to grow on.

3 *It is important to have these new shoots on the canes in the next growing season because they will keep the canes alive while more are being sent up from the buds on the roots.*

Fall raspberries

The fall-fruiting raspberries extend the fresh fruit season well into the fall - until the first frosts, in fact. They crop as heavily as the summer varieties, but over a longer period. As well as fruiting on the new canes, another difference is that they are much more vigorous. You must, therefore, keep the width of a row to no more than 18in(45cm) from one side to the other.

Left: Fall raspberries need no permanent support. Pass some twine down both sides of the row and secure it at each end.

Right: 'Autumn Bliss' is a superb fall variety and provides fresh fruit until the first frosts put a stop to cropping.

Above: The early and popular summer raspberry 'Glen Clova'. A regular and heavy cropper, with medium-sized berries of good flavor.

Below: A good stand of strong, new canes after pruning. Tie them to the supporting wires with soft twine to leave them about 4in(10cm) apart.

Above: If, after tying in, the tops of the new canes reach well above the top wire, bend them over carefully and tie them down to prevent damage.

Below: Prune summer raspberries straight after fruiting. Cut out all the canes that have fruited, along with any new ones that appear weak.

Blackberries and hybrid cane fruits

Since the introduction of improved thornless varieties, blackberries have become more popular as a garden fruit. There are many ways of training blackberries, but with the exception of 'Loch Ness', all methods involve tying the canes to horizontal wires so that they can be tended and picked easily. One feature common to all systems is that the new canes are kept separate - and usually above - those that are about to fruit to reduce the likelihood of diseases being passed from old to new canes. The less vigorous 'Loch Ness' need not be tied to wires; simply train it onto vertical poles about 8ft(2.5m) tall. It is a good variety for small gardens.

With very few exceptions, hybrid cane fruits are all hybrids between blackberries and raspberries. Mostly, they have the long, supple canes of the blackberry but, except for the few thornless variants, their numerous small thorns are more like those of the raspberry. Training systems are similar to those for blackberries. Despite the unquestioned hardiness of the parents, hybrids themselves are sometimes damaged by a hard winter, so in cold areas take the precaution of tying the new canes together in a bundle before the winter and only release them for tying in properly when the worst weather is past. The bundled canes protect each other. Like blackberries, prune the hybrid berries by cutting out the fruited canes soon after fruiting is over. Hybrid cane fruits include the tasty loganberry, the tayberry, sunberry, marionberry, boysenberry and the recently introduced tummelberry.

Although ripe enough for making jellies, these fruits are not yet fit for dessert; they should be darker.

Right: *Once established, the tayberry is a very heavy cropper. Crops are up to twice the weight of the loganberry and the plants are hardier. The straw mulch suppresses weeds and helps the soil to retain adequate moisture.*

Left: *The tayberry is one of the comparatively new race of hybrids. They are similar in flavor, but vary in hardiness, vigor and appearance.*

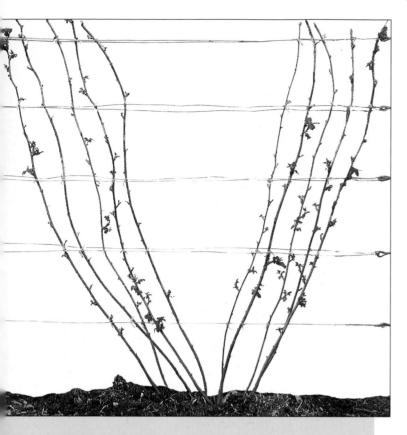

Above: *For less vigorous hybrids, such as this loganberry, a fan system of training is ideal. The new canes are trained up the gap in the center between next year's fruiting canes.*

Above: *The 'Oregon Thornless' blackberry is one of the tastiest thornless varieties and a most attractive plant, with its deeply cut leaves. It is quite vigorous.*

Above: *'Fantasia' is immensely vigorous and thorny, but crops prodigiously and has an excellent flavor. It freezes well, but some berries are apt to go red on freezing.*

Right: *Some of the most vigorous blackberries produce only one or two new canes each year. To fill the allotted space, nip out the top of the new canes when they are 5ft(1.5m) tall to induce side shoots to form. This increases the length of fruiting cane and, therefore, also the crop.*

Part Three

GROWING HERBS

Herbs are fairly easy to please - after all, most of them grow vigorously in the wild and some may even be classed as wildflowers or weeds. You will find that the majority need little more than a sunny situation and a free-draining soil; most will not thrive in waterlogged ground at any rate. There are exceptions of course: herbs such as bogbean grow naturally beside ponds and streams, while woodland plants, such as woodruff, prefer shade; these will be useful for those difficult spots in the garden. It does pay to find out which conditions your herbs prefer and to accommodate them as closely as possible. That way, your plants are more likely to flourish and produce the healthiest, best-looking results. Another factor you will want to consider is the size of each plant, and herbs offer plenty of variety for tubs and borders alike. Some species, such as angelica and fennel, grow to well over 48in(120cm) tall, while others, including thyme and chamomile, are ground-huggers that produce a delightful carpet effect. Herbs can be chosen for hedging - rosemary and santolina, for example, are ideal and can also be clipped into formal effects - or grown as an ornamental tree, such as bay, or as shrubs - juniper, myrtle and witch hazel are good examples. Then there is the wonderful range of colors to choose from: silver-leaved herbs, such as southernwood or santolina; the purple hues of fennels, sages and basils; the golden glow of marjoram and thyme; the bright reds, blues and yellows of bergamot, borage and marigold. Many herbs have attractive variegated foliage, too.

Left: A thyme seat makes a magnificent focal point in any garden. *Right: A sprig of angelica.*

101

BAD PLANT

Avoid plants like this one, with large areas of bare stem and dead foliage. Weeds in the pot are also competing for precious nutrients.

Choosing a good plant

To grow herbs successfully, it is important to start with a good, healthy plant and to plant it correctly. Always buy your plants from a good garden center or, better still, from a specialist nursery where you can obtain expert information and advice. Check the plants over thoroughly and avoid any that are limp and drooping, with sparse stems and just a few pale or discolored leaves. Look closely for any signs of disease or insect infestation and make sure that the soil has not dried out and shrunk away from the sides of the pot. If there is a mat of roots protruding from the base, this a sign that the plant is rootbound and should have been repotted long ago. Having chosen a healthy specimen, take it home carefully. Carry it upright at all times and protect it from the risk of pieces breaking off. Do not leave it in a hot, airless vehicle for any length of time. When you arrive home, take it outside straightaway and water it thoroughly before planting as soon as possible. Herbs are not difficult to grow; they are tolerant of most conditions and, being strongly flavored, they are not particularly attractive to slugs, snails and other pests. Given good conditions, you can achieve impressive results in a single season.

GOOD PLANT

A healthy plant such as this has shape and vigor, with plenty of leaves right down to the base of the stem.

BAD PLANT

This plant has not been pinched out at the top, so has grown too long and leggy before keeling over.

GOOD PLANT

Choose this one in preference; it is compact and bushy, with a good shape.

BAD PLANT

Do not make the mistake of going for the larger plant because you think it is better value. This long, leggy plant may be in flower, but it has very little foliage on weak-looking stems and a mass of roots protruding from the base of the pot.

GOOD PLANT

This good, compact little plant with a tight head of healthy foliage will grow quickly and well, once it is transplanted to the herb garden or patio container.

BAD PLANT

This stunted specimen has far too little foliage on its woody stems and a great deal of dead material.

GOOD PLANT

By contrast, this specimen has a good shape, plenty of healthy-looking leaves around a central stem and a flower spike is beginning to form. Good-quality stock will ensure a successful garden or an impressive display, providing you continue to look after it correctly.

103

Herbs for sunny places

Few gardens have perfect soil and the ideal conditions for all the herbs you might wish to grow. Fortunately, there are plants that will flourish in a wide variety of soils and situations. Hot dry areas of the garden will suit many plants and you can help the soil to retain sufficient moisture by mulching it with a top dressing of potting mixture, gravel, bark or similar material. A garden that is full of sunshine and has plenty of moisture at root level will suit many herbs. Here we look at a range of herbs that will flourish in sunny areas of your garden.

Sun worshippers

The leaves of creeping and bushy varieties of thyme provide a variety of textures and patterns, especially when covered with dew or frost. There are many varieties of lavender, with flowers that range from pale blue to deep purple, white to deep pink. Dry, sunny gardens are ideal for the gray-leaved curry plant, with its bright yellow flowers and curry-like aroma. Use to garnish soups and egg dishes. The pretty members of the hyssop family develop flowers from midsummer onwards, attracting bees and butterflies. Rock hyssop has rich, blue, upright flowers. Other varieties have pink, blue, purple or white flowers. The larger hyssops tend to bend with the weight of flowers and look beautiful on raised beds and banks. Do not forget the marjoram family, the many purple, green and variegated sages, aromatic winter savory and rosemary - if you have space in your garden.

The sweet, spicy gray-green leaves of alecost, also known as costmary, may be used in stuffings and potpourri.

The long-lasting, pretty pink flowers of calamint are enhanced by bright green scented leaves.

The gray-green foliage of lavender always looks attractive, especially when smothered in flower spikes from summer onwards.

Few cats can resist the smell of catnip, a tall, gray-leaved plant with white flowers. Dry the leaves and stalks to make catnip mice.

Once established, most of the thyme family will cover a dry bank and provide color from spring until midsummer.

HERBS FOR DAMP, SUNNY PLACES

Damp sunbathers

Angelica needs damp soil to grow tender stalks for crystallizing. The leaves and stalks of this biennial plant are at their best in the first year. Coriander also thrives in sunny, damp locations. Because the plant bolts into flower, cut the leaves while young and pull out the plant when the 'carroty' leaves develop. The leaves of self heal form a useful ground cover mat. It has deep blue, 4in(10cm)-tall flowers. Bergamot, with its red, white, pink or purple flowers, is good for flavoring tea. Mace (Achillea declorans) has white flowerheads and leaves with a flavor reminiscent of the tropical spice of the same name.

Add small pieces of angelica leaf and stalk to fruit during cooking for a delicate fragrance and flavor.

Fresh carraway leaf is mild. For many centuries, the seeds were taken to relieve indigestion. Today they are used for flavoring many foods and pickles.

Remove the flowering heads of salad burnet to encourage tender new leaves for adding to salads.

In damp soil, comfrey produces abundant leaves for cropping and a profusion of beautiful flowers in a range of colors.

The strong, celery, yeasty flavor of lovage enhances many soups and stews, especially if they contain carrots. Use young leaves in salads.

Add young, tender rocket leaves to salads and eastern dishes. The pale cream flowers have a delicious mustard flavor.

Plant marsh mallow at the back of the border; it may grow to 6.5ft(2m) before the pale pink flowers open in late summer.

105

Herbs for shady places

Having a shady garden is no bar to growing a variety of herbs. Many prefer dappled shade and a well-drained soil, especially those with light or golden variegation on the leaves. Curly gold marjoram, golden marjoram, golden sage and variegated melissa (lemon balm) are good examples. All are excellent culinary herbs, but exposure to direct sunshine all day may spoil their appearance by browning the edges of the leaves. If you have an area of damp shade in your garden, the bright golden leaves of golden feverfew and golden meadowsweet, with its spires of fluffy white flowers in late spring, will provide bright splashes of color. Dry shade may seem to pose more of a problem, but do not despair; you can allow the pretty, variegated herb ground elder to take over! Periwinkles (*Vinca*) also flourish in dry shade. *V. major variegata* produces a bushy mass of leathery, evergreen leaves splashed with butter yellow that grow to 12in(30cm) or more high. The new growth in early spring is covered with sky blue flowers over many weeks. The lesser periwinkle varieties have silver-edged or gold-edged green leaves and blue flowers and provide useful ground cover, even in hostile situations. The humble ground ivy makes a pretty ground cover, with musky scented leaves and blue flowers.

Below: Golden feverfew retains its bright gold leaf color in the shade. Deadhead regularly to encourage fresh flowers to develop until the fall.

Dappled shade

*The lemony acid leaves of French sorrel (*Rumex acetosa*) and buckler sorrel (R. scutatus) will be more tender when grown in shade. Bugle (Ajuga reptans) is a good ground cover when edging a shady border. Many varieties have beautifully colored leaves and rich blue flowers. Golden feverfew produces a mass of bright green leaves and pretty white single or double flowers from spring to the fall. It has proved very helpful to migraine sufferers. Other herbs found at the edge of woodlands include primrose, wild strawberries, St. John's wort, foxgloves and valerian.*

French sorrel (Rumex acetosa)

Curly gold marjoram (Origanum vulgare aureum crispum)

Bugle (Ajuga reptans 'Burgundy Glow')

106

HERBS FOR DAMP SHADE

Ginger mint (Mentha x gentilis '*Variegata*')

Curled parsley (Petroselinum crispum)

Corsican mint (Mentha requienii)

Pennyroyal (Mentha pulegium)

Lady's mantle (Alchemilla mollis)

Golden feverfew (Tanacetum parthenium aureum)

Right: *Damp shade will encourage ginger mint (Mentha x gentilis 'Variegata') to produce long red stems carrying blue 'puffball' flowers between the spicy green-and-gold leaves. Cut regularly for new growth.*

Damp shade

Curled and plain-leaved varieties of parsley are slow to bolt into flower in shade, but need rich, moist soil to thrive. Creeping and upright pennyroyal spreads into a carpet of scented leaves along paths and banks. Gingermint, with its spicy green-and-gold leaf variegation, has pale blue flowers on upright stems from early summer until the fall. Other suitable herbs include flat-leaved golden marjoram, sweet and dog violets, celandine, centaury and hedge hyssop.

107

Herbs that thrive near water

Plants vary in their ability to live in really 'wet' soil. Many will flourish, but some may not survive if the water is stagnant, so it is far better if there is some flow of fresh water. There are various ways of improving the soil conditions: one solution is raising a bed so that the plants can send down taproots for water while leaving the rest of their roots in drained soil. Wet clay soil can be improved by installing proper drainage pipes and introducing plenty of grit and bulky natural compost. All these measures help to provide the air spaces in the soil that plants require in addition to water. Many beautiful herbs will thrive in damp, even marshy, situations, producing a succession of flowers in a wide range of colors.

A seaside garden will thrive if there are sheltering walls and hedges to provide protection from a strong prevailing wind, especially in winter. Overhead watering to wash off salt deposits helps plants to recover after stormy weather. Many people have created beautiful coastal gardens using herbs of all kinds - sheltered garden 'rooms' with their own microclimate.

The bright golden-yellow flowers of Elecampane (Inula helenium), which can grow up to 6.5ft(2m) high, are very dramatic in a large garden.

Meadowsweet (Filipendula), with its clouds of fluffy white flowers on slender stalks, has flat rosettes of green, gold or variegated green-gold leaves.

Below: Moist soil encourages sweet cicely to produce a mass of ferny, anise-scented leaves. Tiny white spots on the leaves are no cause for alarm - they are characteristic of the plant.

Unimproved wild forms of comfrey (Symphytum) are usually found by water. Dwarf forms are available for small gardens.

Marsh mallow (Althaea officinalis) needs moist soil to produce edible tender young shoots and roots. The confection is made from the root extract.

HERBS FOR THE SEASIDE

Evening primrose (Oenothera biennis) flourishes by the coast. The scented flowers open each night. Some improved varieties retain open flowers all day.

Herbs with wet feet

For an interesting contrast of flower color and leaf shape, try planting purple loosestrife, with its upright foliage and flowers, spiky figwort, which has unusual tiny red-fringed flowers, and pink soapwort. Sweet cicely is pretty all year round, with its soft, ferny, aromatic leaves and white flowers, followed by large mahogany-colored seeds. In a large garden, self-supporting Joe Pye weed, or gravelroot, (Eupatorium purpureum) is a real talking point. A carefully planned seaside garden could enjoy a range of lavender flowers from early summer until late fall.

Bay (Laurus nobilis) enjoys salty air, but must be sheltered from cold winds.

The yellow to cream button flowers of cotton lavender (Santolina) would brighten any garden.

Aromatic, colorful sage makes good ground cover. Trim the tips of the shoots during the growing season so that plants remain bushy.

Thrift is a seaside plant often seen on clifftops. The pink flowers rise from flat cushions of leaves. There are many attractive cultivated varieties in several colors for the garden.

Rosemary (Rosmarinus officinalis) literally means 'dew of the sea'. It will flourish in a seaside atmosphere, providing it is warm and well sheltered from cold winds in winter.

109

Herbs for chalk and clay

Chalk is usually an easy soil to work with, but it does need plenty of humus to build up the nutrients and improve the water retention. In the case of heavy clay soils, it is a good idea to leave them weeded but 'rough' in the fall to allow frost to break down the clumps. Dig in rough, gritty compost when the soil is workable to improve the texture. Most herbs can be encouraged to grow in a range of unusual situations, but some really prefer a chalk soil. Red and green fennel, with their tall, feathery fronds and yellow flowers, provide plenty of leaves for cooking and are known to aid the digestion. Use the dried stalks to flavor fish and barbecue dishes. Borage also thrives on chalk, and the plants are usually humming with a wide variety of bees. Cut chives and garlic chives as new growth appears to provide delicious leaves and flowers for salads. The warm pink to deep purple flowers of marjoram seem more vibrant when the plant is growing on a chalk soil. All the origanum family are worth gathering and drying for winter use; there are many variations in flavor from sweet and mild to a biting pungent warmth.

Below: In spring, support the rapid, lush growth of comfrey. The flowers appear soon after and will be buzzing with bees.

Above: Be sure to plant horseradish in an area that it can safely colonize. It is pungent and delicious in sauces and the leaves are useful in 'bath bags' to ease aching joints after gardening.

Herbs that thrive in clay soil

Comfrey	Symphytum officinale
Elecampane	Inula helenium
Golden rod	Solidago virgaurea
Joe Pye weed	Eupatorium purpureum
Hemp agrimony	E. p. roseum
Horseradish	Armoracia rusticana
Jacob's ladder	Polemonium caeruleum
Tansy	Tanacetum vulgare

Fresh or dried, the firm stalks and flat golden flowerheads of tansy (here the curly variety) make it popular with flower arrangers.

Herbs for chalky soil

Most herbs prefer a neutral to alkaline soil, rather than an acid one, so it is worth experimenting with a range of herbs and mulching well. Suitable plants for chalky soil also include:

Pasque flower
Russian sage
Mullein
Juniper
Flax
Scabious
Dyer's chamomile
Toadflax
Wild wallflower

Left: *In spring, the deep purple flowerbuds of chives open to a brighter purple and then fade to pale pink. The florets of young flowers add flavor and color to salads. Remove faded flowers to encourage new leaf growth and flowers. If left to ripen, gather the seeds when they become black and hard.*

Chives (Allium schoenoprasum) *are attractive in groups or as an edging.*

The sky-blue flowers of borage (Borago officinalis) *provide plenty of edible flowers for drinks and salads.*

Oregano (Origanum vulgare) *develops a warm, pungent flavor to enhance Italian, French and Greek food.*

A garden would be incomplete without the useful evergreen leaves and pretty flowers of culinary thyme (Thymus vulgaris).

Compact marjoram (Origanum compactum)

Bronze fennel (Foeniculum vulgare purpurascens)

111

Summer maintenance

Herbs are generally easy to maintain, even in summer. Most aromatic herbs tolerate dry, sunny conditions and a poor, stony soil, while woodland herbs flourish in the kind of damp, shady positions many other garden plants abhor. Most herbs are rampant growers, spreading thick and fast during a single season, giving weeds no chance. Good ground cover means minimum watering, too. All but the moisture-loving herbs can survive with little or no watering, even in prolonged hot conditions. The only exception applies to herbs in containers, where the soil dries out more quickly. Here, regular watering is essential - but good drainage too, as herbs hate a waterlogged soil even more than a parched one. Patio and windowbox herbs will need regular feeding. Try to use an organic fertilizer, preferably a herbal feed, such as an infusion of nettles, yarrow, coltsfoot or comfrey. Heavily cropped garden herbs also benefit from an occasional feed during the growing season. Herbs do not really suffer much from insect attacks. An infusion of basil, elder or garlic with a spoonful of washing-up liquid or soft soap will deal with aphids; dried herbs, such as sage, can be sprinkled around plants to deter mildew, slugs and snails. Some shrubby herbs in formal herb gardens may need trimming during the summer.

Below: Add powdered fertilizers to the water or use a powdered herb, such as chamomile or sage, to protect seedlings and young plants from damping off.

Right: Tomato fertilizer is fine for herbs. You can also make up a strong infusion of garlic and dilute it with water to deter caterpillars, aphids and flea beetles from mature plants. Be sure to label all storage bottles clearly.

Left: *A mulch of small stones around young plants helps conserve moisture and deters weeds. Pull out weeds in spring while the herbs are establishing themselves and you should have no problems later on.*

Below: *Bark chips make an excellent mulch, as they are attractive to look at and eventually rot down to enrich the soil with valuable compost.*

Left: *Plant lush-growing herbs in close profusion and watering will become an infrequent chore. When watering, take the opportunity to add a herbal fertilizer, such as nettle or comfrey tea.*

Above: *Deadheading flowering herbs throughout the summer encourages new blooms. If the herbs are being grown to harvest the leaves, remove the flowerbuds before they open.*

Cutting back and tidying up

Like all vigorous perennial plants, herbs begin to look straggly or outgrow their allotted space at the end of each growing season. Even though you have been cropping plants for the kitchen or for drying, there will still be dead flowerheads to remove and diseased or damaged foliage to snip away. Older plants also tend to become woody or shapeless after a while. By cutting or pinching off dead or shriveled leaves, you also discourage disease and prevent a proliferation of slugs and snails. Cut back any dead or straggly stems almost to soil level. This may seem a little drastic, but will encourage stronger, more vigorous growth and a healthier plant. Trim small, mat-forming plants, such as thyme, with a pair of sharp kitchen scissors but use secateurs for taller, shrubby herbs, such as lavender, tansy and santolina, or even hedging shears for mature growth. In the informal garden, an annual cut-back and trim to remove unsightly stems and help plants to keep their shape, will suffice. The formal herb garden requires a little more thought and effort, particularly where a low hedging herb, such as box, lavender or rosemary, has been trimmed to create knot designs or geometric topiary shapes. Mulching between plants with colored pebbles or bark helps to maintain the desired shape of each herb. While plants are young and still being shaped, they may need trimming several times a year. To speed up the thickening process, prune out any strong woody branches growing horizontally from the main shape, trimming them back into the main canopy of the plant.

1 In late summer, trim back the old flower stalks, top twigs and shoots of tall, shrubby plants, such as this Lavandula spica 'Munstead'.

2 Keep the plant outline slightly rounded in shape to help it shed heavy rain or snow during winter. Reduce the plant by two-thirds.

3 In spring, remove any winter-damaged twigs or branches to ensure a fine summer display of flowers on the neatened bushes.

Left: *Encourage bushy growth of gray foliage on cotton lavender by cutting back all long, thin branches to a shoot just above the level of the mature wood in late winter or early spring. Keep the base wider than the top.*

Right: *Remove the dead flowers and untidy growth from bushy thymes in the fall. In spring, cut out dead and weak growth to encourage new shoots from healthy wood. Fill the center of the plant with a little fine potting mix to encourage rooting from the stems.*

Below: *Every year, remove excessive growth from rue to encourage the beautiful blue mound of leaves. Cut back to just above the mature wood where new shoots are visible. Wear gloves; rue may irritate sensitive skin.*

Below: *Every year, remove the top growth of tansy by cutting off the dead stalks close to the ground, just above any new, developing leaves. Do the same with fennel, French tarragon, lovage and woodruff.*

Only trim the tips of the branches on young sage plants. With older plants, you can cut off the top third to prevent them becoming straggly and shapeless.

Above: *All sages, including this purple sage, Salvia officinalis purpurescens, should be trimmed back in early spring to encourage plenty of new shoots with good leaf coloration.*

Propagating herbs by seed

Growing herb plants from seed has several advantages: annual varieties can be replaced every year, there are considerable cost savings if you are planning, say, a hedge or lawn, and you will have access to a far wider variety of herb species and varieties. Most specialist herb seed stockists will mail supplies to their customers. The disadvantages are that, as with any plants grown from seed, you cannot guarantee that the new plants will be identical to the parent. Also, you may be left with many surplus plants, although you can usually sell or exchange these. The easiest way to sow seed is to sprinkle it directly onto the ground, preferably once the risk of frost is over. It helps if the soil is finely raked and free from weeds. A glass or plastic cloche over the seedbed protects young seedlings. Annual varieties with a long growing season are best started off indoors. This method is more reliable, as you can control the growing conditions, such as soil, temperature and light. You may even consider buying a purpose-made propagator to keep seeds ideally protected, ventilated and heated. To avoid the risk of 'damping off' - a condition in which young seedlings die off - use a sterilized potting mixture. White mold on the surface of the soil is a warning sign of this fungal infection. Watering with a weak infusion of chamomile can sometimes halt the condition before it progresses too far.

1 Small individual pots may be made of biodegradable fiber or reusable plastic. Fill them with a sterilized potting mix and water well.

2 Sprinkle a few seeds into each pot, using your fingertips for fine seeds. If the seeds are larger, press a couple of them lightly into the surface of the soil.

3 Arrange the pots in a propagating tray and top with a fine layer of vermiculite or sterilized potting mix, sprinkling it with your fingers to avoid making the layer too thick. Water lightly.

4 Plant up larger trays in the same way, providing they have suitable drainage holes. Fill with about 1.6in (4cm) of sterilized seed potting mix, moisten well and sprinkle with seed.

Carefully label all pots and trays for future reference.

5 Finish off with a fine layer of vermiculite or seed mix. Use an empty pot for better control over larger areas. Moisten with tepid water.

6 Cover the tray with paper, glass or a ventilated plastic cover. Leave it in a warm place or turn on the heat if the propagator is an electrically operated model.

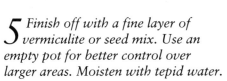

7 Check the trays and pots every day or two and make sure the soil remains moist. Move them to a light situation as soon as the first seedlings appear.

When the seedlings are large enough to handle, prick them out carefully into a deeper seed tray or peat pots.

117

Taking soft semi-ripe cuttings

1 *This bushy branch of red sage will provide plenty of material for cuttings. Examine it for signs of disease or pests and remove any thrips or whitefly by washing under running water. Select healthy, undamaged young branches.*

Many plants, including sage, marjoram, pineapple sage and lavender - in fact almost any herb that you wish to increase - will root well from cuttings taken at any time from late spring to early summer. Select healthy shoots at the right stage of growth, i.e. when the current season's shoots start to harden at the base. Test the shoot between your fingers. If it breaks, the shoot is either too soft or too hard. If it springs back when you let go, the shoot is at the right stage. On sage plants, as with many other herbs, the central growth on each branch is usually more advanced than the side shoots. Selecting this stem for propagation will encourage a bushy, attractive plant. If you are propagating from one of the colored sages (golden, purple or variegated), make certain that you select the shoot with the best coloration on the plant. In this way, you can be sure of maintaining good, well-colored plant stock. Remove any excess leaves on the stems, leaving about two leaves below the central leaf tips. If the cutting has too many leaves, it has to work to keep them firm with moisture. This can delay or prevent the more important task of forming roots for the new plant.

2 *Start by removing the lower leaves to expose the stem. Usually a gentle tug is all that is needed, but you can use a sharp knife for the task if necessary.*

3 *Remove all the leaves on the stem except for the tip leaf buds and the two leaves beneath. This will expose the soft new season's growth.*

4 *Cut through the stem at the point where the 'wood' is beginning to harden, just above the small stalks of the previous year's growth.*

5 *Make a hole with a dibble and insert the cuttings. These cuttings are being placed into pots, but a deep seed tray is just as suitable. Rooting in pots allows the cuttings plenty of room for root growth. Cuttings in trays will need to be potted on at an earlier stage, once rooting is established.*

Use a potting mixture with an open, gritty texture.

This dibble is custom-made, but the blunt end of a pen or pencil will serve equally well.

Propagating from soft woody cuttings

Rosemary, cotton lavenders, golden rod and many of the aromatic artemisias will root from soft, mature wood taken as cuttings during the summer and fall. Be adventurous and take cuttings from any plant, as long as it is free from disease and will not miss some of its growth. Strip the cutting of the lower leaves and cut the base at an angle to extend the area of soft bark, as this is where the roots will form. Insert the cutting into a tray or pot containing good-quality, open 'gritty' soil. Fine gravel, vermiculite and perlite are all suitable for cuttings. Work as quickly as possible; more cuttings die from delay, drying out and rough handling than from any other cause. Check the soil every day to make sure there is sufficient moisture, but do not overwater. Provide warmth at soil level if possible. Once rooted, all cuttings should be 'potted on' into individual pots with good-quality soil, as they will rapidly take up valuable nutrients.

The new season's soft stem growth appears as you remove the leaves.

2 *Carefully pull the leaves from the shoot to expose the soft green stem. Leave the leading main shoot at the tip and two or three small groups of leaves below the leader.*

1 *Select healthy side branches with plenty of new growth. A gentle pull sideways will usually separate the shoot from the main stem.*

3 Trim the cutting, making a clean cut across the young green stem. Keep the cut ends moist with a damp cloth if you have a lot of cuttings to prepare.

4 Insert the cutting until the lower leaves are almost touching the soil and firm it gently with the finger to ensure that no air pockets are left. The cutting should be upright and completely in contact with the soil.

Use a sharp knife to make a clean cut. Ragged ends may encourage rotting and disease.

If you are interrupted while planting cuttings and cannot finish immediately, place the cuttings in a sealed plastic bag and keep them overnight in the vegetable section of a refrigerator.

121

Taking tip cuttings from small plants

Small, shrubby plants, such as thyme, grow soft tips and stems from the woody, mature growth made during the previous season. These tips will root easily if taken between early summer and the onset of fall. Select a suitable bunch of soft growth from the garden plant and place it immediately in a plastic bag out of direct sunshine to prevent any loss of moisture from the leaves. Label each bag if you are taking cuttings from different plants, as it can be difficult to identify them later. The soil for cuttings must be gritty to provide plenty of spaces for air and water to percolate, and free-draining, to encourage rapid root growth. Rooting will take place in four to six weeks in a covered, heated propagator. It will be slower, but just as successful, if you support a plastic bag with three or more sticks or wire hoops over the tray. When new growth appears, ventilate the bag with a few holes, gradually increasing the number of holes over several days, before removing the bag completely.

2 Thoroughly water the tray about two hours before planting to allow excess water to drain away. Insert the cuttings 2in(5cm) apart in a tray or put 4-6 cuttings in a 4in(10cm) pot.

1 Trim pieces to 2-3in (5-7.5cm) by cutting through the semi-soft stem above a woody section. Remove the lower leaves.

Cut off young shoots with a sharp knife.

3 *Always label the finished tray with the plant name and date, especially if you have taken plenty of cuttings. A final mist spray will refresh the leaves and also helps to 'settle' the soil.*

Cuttings from different plants can share the same tray, as long as their aftercare is similar.

Rooted cuttings

After four weeks, the simple cuttings of thyme shown at the far lefthand side of the photograph have started to develop. The soil has been shaken off the cuttings on the righthand side to show the first fine roots. Most roots develop at the base, but a few may grow from the sides. When lifting rooted cuttings from the seed tray or pots, try to retain as much undisturbed soil as possible, as this encourages quick, healthy growth when the cuttings are potted on.

4 *Cover the propagator with the lid, leaving the vents open. Put it in a warm place, such as under the staging of a greenhouse, but out of the sun.*

Propagating herbs from root divisions

Many perennial herbs can be successfully propagated by dividing the roots to create new plants. The best time to do this is in the fall or early spring after the foliage has died down or withered. Root division is not only the simplest and cheapest way of acquiring new plants, it also regenerates the parent plant and prevents it growing too large. Providing the soil is not frozen or waterlogged, dig up the whole plant very carefully, using a couple of garden forks as a lever if the plant is big and well established. Lever the fork into the ground beside the plant and loosen the soil on all sides before attempting to lift it. Ease the soil from the roots, taking care not to damage them - washing with water can be a useful way to clean off dried or stubborn soil. Then gently tease the roots apart with your hands (protected with gloves if necessary) or use a garden fork and a sharp knife if the roots are tough or badly tangled.

Now is a good opportunity for you to check for any signs of disease or infestation, which you should cut away and burn before it spreads. After pulling apart the new, individual plants, lay them out, making sure that each section includes healthy roots and strong growth buds. Trim away any dead material and replant the new plants as soon as possible, at the same depth.

Another advantage of vegetative propagation, such as root division, is that it enables you to produce plants that are identical to the parent - something that cannot be guaranteed when growing from seed. This method is particularly suited to herbaceous plants with creeping roots and stems, such as mint, tansy and tarragon, and for herbs grown from bulbs, such as chives. With these, the clumps of tiny bulbils are easy to separate and replant at the correct depth.

1 *This chive is about three years old and just starting into new leaf growth. This is a good time to lift and divide it into several new plants to replant into an attractive group or row.*

Dividing large herb plants

Large herbs, such as comfrey, will often have developed large roots that break when you lift them. Discard any old wood - this is usually near the center of the plant - and trim off any large, broken or diseased roots to prevent them rotting in the ground. You can then begin to divide up the remaining segment into several smaller, more manageable pieces, each with its own strong root system and viable growth buds.

Divide chive
plants in the
spring or fall.

3 Use your hands to tease the
chives apart. They will divide
naturally into small groups of bulbils
that are easy to replant.

Dividing French marjoram

Trim off hard stalks and
old growth. Separate and
break the clump into
small plants, complete
with roots. The roots and
new growth are clustered
around the base of the old
stalks. Discard any old or
very woody pieces.

A big clump of chives may
require the leverage of two
forks to break it apart.

2 Divide the plant, using a fork if
necessary, and loosen the soil
around the roots. Clumps of chives
will need dividing and transplanting
every three or four years.

Aromatic herbs

Since all herbs are naturally aromatic, to grow them is to create a scented garden automatically - heady with mingled scents on a sunny day as the heat of the sun releases all those essential oils, but even more wonderful after a quick summer shower. But if a fragrant garden or backyard is your primary intention, then you can select your plants specifically for their sweetness and compatibility of scent. Old-fashioned moss roses are an obvious starting point, the perfect companion for so many of the traditional cottage garden and herb plants, such as garden pinks, sweet william, stocks, lavenders and thymes. Plant bushy herbs, such as lavender, hyssop, bergamot and rosemary, in beds close to seating or paths where you will naturally brush against them. Keep marjorams, calamints, lemon balm, lemon verbena and chamomile in pots, tubs and raised beds where they are accessible. Creeping thymes and prostrate chamomiles are ideal underfoot; they will release their scents as they are trodden on. There are many bonuses to a scented garden: the wonderful range of shapes and colors, the beautiful flowers, and all the bees and butterflies they will attract.

Above: Spicy scented hyssop is one of the ingredients in eau-de-cologne. It has light green, narrow leaves and usually blue flowers, although this is a pretty pink variety. Attracts butterflies.

Left: Lemon balm, with its strong, fresh fragrance, is attractive in the bed or border. Harvest the leaves to make refreshing tisanes, a scented bath or add them to salads, sauces and fruits.

Right: Aromatic French marjoram makes a large clump of vigorous foliage, with pink buds and white flowers. It was once used to make small scented bags and toilet waters.

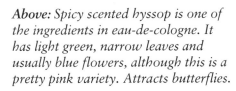

Hyssop
(Hyssopus officinalis)

Oregano
(Origanum
vulgare)

Anise hyssop
(Agastache anethiodora)

Nepeta
'Six Hills Giant'

A scented garden

You can create many types of scented garden, depending on the mood or environment you wish to evoke. A Mediterranean herb garden might remind you of sunny, summer holidays or perhaps you want to recapture the past, with a heady mixture of old-fashioned flowers and herbs. Alternatively, you could establish a butterfly garden, a potpourri garden or perhaps even a night-scented garden.

Pot marjoram
(Origanum onites)

Variegated calamint
(Calamintha grandiflora variegata)

Nepeta grandiflora

Greater calamint
(Calamintha grandiflora)

Lavandula angustifolia
'Hidcote'

Thyme in patios and paving

Thyme is a most useful garden plant. Its tiny leaves and dense habit create a carpet, cushion or low hedge according to variety, and are ideal for softening harder landscaped features, such as walls, paths and the edges of containers. The most commonly seen species in the wild and in the garden is *Thymus vulgaris,* a shrubby perennial about 12in(30cm) high with tiny gray-green leaves and a mass of small white or mauve flowers. The creeping thyme, *Thymus serpyllum,* grows wild in Europe and can be planted among alpines in the rockery or in the cracks between the paving stones and slabs of a path or patio, where your feet will brush against the leaves, releasing a warm, pungent scent. The more upright varieties can be clipped into low, compact hedges, ideal for edging beds and borders or a formal herb garden design. There is a range of types and flavors to choose from, including gold and silver varieties such as 'Golden Lemon' and 'Silver Posie', which look lovely grown together in a thyme bed or contrasted with other herb shapes and colors. Lemon thyme, *Thymus x citriodorus,* is popular with cooks, ideal for adding to rich stews and stuffings. It has rounded green leaves and pale pink flowers and makes a compact, low mound of fresh, lemon-scented foliage.

Different varieties of thyme add color and interest to a bank in the garden.

Left: Thymus fragrantissimus *makes a dense dome of pale mauve flowers. Position it on a corner or close to a path to encourage the wonderfully fragrant scent to be released whenever anyone brushes past it.*

Growing thyme

Thyme can be propagated by seed, cuttings, layering or root division. To grow it from seed, sow it in early spring and plant out or thin to 10in(25cm) apart in well-drained soil. Thyme will thrive in any well-drained, sunny position and you should be able to crop it all year round, unless winter frosts are severe, in which case protect it with straw or soil. Harvest the leaves for drying just as the flower buds are opening by cutting the stems to about 2in(5cm) from the ground. Thyme is also an excellent bee plant.

Thymus vulgaris *is the most commonly grown species and often used in cooking.*

Left: *Different varieties of thyme make a dense carpet of tiny aromatic leaves and flowers, ideal for stony outcrops, steps, stone walls and rocky slopes. The patchwork of plants also helps to bind the thin soil together.*

Right: *A creeping variety of thyme is perfect for growing between patio slabs or alongside a path or stepping stones. It spreads and softens the edges of the stones and can survive being trodden on occasionally.*

1 *To plant a creeping thyme beside a path or in between paving stones, first hollow out a planting pocket in the soil the right size for the plant.*

2 *Press the plant firmly into the soil, leaving no gaps around the rootball. All the foliage should remain on the surface and not be half-buried.*

3 *Label the thyme if you wish. It will soon spread. The many varieties include a lemon-scented and a gray-leaved, woolly form.*

Rosemary for edging

It is said that where rosemary flourishes, a woman wears the trousers. In fact, it grows abundantly in the wild in Mediterranean countries and will do well in any sunny, sheltered site with a light, well-drained soil. In a northern climate, growing rosemary in a large, well-drained tub or container may be equally successful, providing the plant can be overwintered under glass. Given ideal conditions, rosemary will grow as high as 6.5ft(2m), and is a useful and decorative evergreen at the rear or center of herb or Mediterranean themed gardens. Its pungent, narrow leaves grow on woody stems, the dark green leaves have silvery undersides and the flowers, which cluster along spiked stems and appear from early spring to early summer, are many shades of blue, as well as pink and white. The plant is easy to propagate from seed or cuttings, layering or root division and needs very little attention to grow into a large, upright, rather shaggy shrub similar to lavender. However, it is also a good plant for trimming and shaping and may be grown as a hedge or formal edging plant around herb beds as an alternative to box, thyme or santolina. Place individual plants about 50cm(20in) apart and trim them immediately after they have flowered. Another alternative to growing rosemary as a focal point in a bed or border, is to train it against a sunny wall.

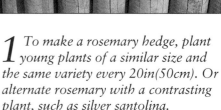

1 *To make a rosemary hedge, plant young plants of a similar size and the same variety every 20in(50cm). Or alternate rosemary with a contrasting plant, such as silver santolina.*

A distinctive flavor

A sprig of pungent rosemary, with its warm, distinctive flavor, is enough to enhance a joint of lamb, a pot of vegetable ratatouille or a barbecue marinade. Use sparingly, as it can turn bitter when taken in excess. Rosemary may be used to complement some desserts too: steep it in the white wine used to make syllabubs or flavor sugar for baking by adding a sprig to the jar.

Rosmarinus
officinalis

Below: *To keep a rosemary bush in shape, trim it immediately after flowering. Snip off straggly younger stems at a natural break in the stem.*

Dry or freeze cuttings

Left: *Rosemary makes a deep green, upright shrub, glossy with essential oils. It will grow as tall as 6.5ft(2m) in a sheltered position, such as against a sunny wall. The spiky leaves have a silvery hue and the stout stems become woody and gnarled with age.*

2 Place young plants into a light, well-drained soil, taking care not to damage stems or roots. Allow each plant to spread itself a little as it settles into its new position.

3 Continue planting. It is a good idea to clear away other plants from the immediate area so that the new ones can establish themselves. A little bark mulch keeps down weeds.

Keep the soil at the same level as it was in the pot.

Keep the plants together for convenience and to make sure you have planted them all.

Above: *A rosemary hedge will establish itself within a couple of seasons. Keep it well trimmed, especially if you want a more formal look. Shape plants after flowering.*

4 Water the plants in thoroughly to encourage the roots to spread out and make good growth. Use rainwater if possible or allow tapwater to stand so that the chlorine can evaporate. Chemicals may harm young plants.

5 Note the details of the herb on a garden tag. If you need to replace one of the plants or wish to extend the hedge in the future, you can then be sure of matching the existing plants.

Tarragon - Mediterranean style

Tarragon, with its tall stems of narrow, bright green pointed leaves, has a wonderful, almost warm aniseed flavor that perfectly complements many dishes, from roast chicken to salad dressings and sauces for egg or fish. French tarragon is preferable, as it has a far superior flavor to the Russian variety and grows to about 39in(1m) high. The flowers are insignificant and rarely open fully in cooler climates, and the seed is not viable, so the plant must be propagated by cuttings or root division. Young plants should be planted out in late spring about 24in(60cm) apart in a sunny position. It is important that the soil is well drained and not too rich. This allows the roots plenty of space to spread, otherwise they will become waterlogged in winter and the plant may not survive. Its preference for a poor, free-draining soil and a sunny site makes tarragon an ideal candidate for a Mediterranean-style planting scheme. To protect the plant from frost in winter, it is a good idea to cut it right down and cover the roots with straw. Potting up a plant and bringing it into the greenhouse at the end of summer will maintain a supply of fresh leaves a little longer. Plants can also be lifted, divided into smaller sections and replanted; if you do this in the spring it will help preserve the flavor of the herb. Tarragon is best used fresh and stems can be cropped throughout the growing period.

3 Remove the tarragon from its pot and lower it gently into the new container, taking care that the roots and stems are undisturbed.

1 Tarragon prefers a well-drained situation. If you plant it in a container, choose one that is made of a porous material, such as terracotta. Cover the drainage hole with pebbles or a crock.

2 Start filling the container with potting mixture - nothing too rich or the tarragon plant will overdo its root growth and take in too much moisture for the winter.

4 Top up the container with potting mixture and firm it gently around the plant, making sure you have left no gaps or air pockets.

5 A sprinkling of gravel or pebbles on the surface of the soil will inhibit weeds and the development of mossy growth.

Harvest fresh leaves all summer.

6 Tarragon will grow to 24-36in (60-90cm) in a container. Unless the site is sheltered, bring the plant under cover for the winter or cut it down and cover the roots with straw.

Thymus drucei minus *with dwarf pinks.*

Bay (Laurus nobilis)

Nepeta *'Six Hills Giant'*

Greek basil (Ocimum minimum *var.* Greek)

Sweet basil (Ocimum basilicum)

French tarragon (Artemisia dracunculus)

French marjoram (Origanum onites x 'French')

Creeping lemon thyme (T. serpyllum *var.*)

Left: *Here, tarragon is just one of the herbs included in a wonderful Mediterranean collection that would look marvelous in the corner of any garden or patio, providing it was sheltered and received plenty of sun.*

133

Planting up a parsley pot

Parsley is probably one of the most used herbs in the kitchen; a vital ingredient in stuffings, marinades and bouquet garnis, and invaluable as a garnish. However, it does not dry well, becoming virtually tasteless, so it is well worth growing it yourself to ensure a fresh supply. Parsley can be chopped and frozen for adding to soups, stews and marinades, but you can still eat it fresh throughout the winter by sowing seeds in the greenhouse in midsummer or potting up the roots of spring-grown plants to bring indoors. Cropping plants by the handful rather than the sprig can quickly outstrip supply if your garden is small. If space is limited, the answer might be multi-pocketed strawberry barrels, which suit parsley just as well and are perfect for backyards and patios. You can buy them in terracotta or plastic; alternatively, make your own from an old wooden barrel. A partly shady spot is ideal for parsley and be sure to provide plenty of moisture. Parsley is a biennial and the leaves taste best in the first year, becoming bitter and rather coarse in the second, so try to sow a fresh supply each year in spring and late summer. The seeds can take at least six weeks to germinate, but this can be speeded up by soaking them overnight in warm water and then soaking a fine tilth seed bed with boiling water before planting. Cover the seeds thinly with fine soil and thin the seedlings to about 10in(25cm) apart.

3 *Once you have released each plant by upturning and tapping the pot, you may need to squeeze the rootball slightly to make it fit through the holes in the parsley pot. Avoid damaging the roots.*

Support the plant gently in your hand as you make it ready for planting.

The dense foliage of curled parsley (Petroselinum crispum) looks best in this kind of container.

1 *Place a few crocks or broken pieces of china in the bottom of the pot to ensure that the drainage holes do not become blocked.*

2 *Fill the pot with potting mix until you nearly reach the level of the planting spaces - in taller pots, these might appear at various heights.*

4 *Insert the parsley plants into the planting holes, pressing them firmly into the potting mixture. Make sure that the rootball is covered and the plants are the right way up.*

5 *Place the final plant in the top of the container, making sure that it is planted at the correct height to grow right out of the top.*

6 *After filling and firming with potting mixture, sprinkle a handful of small stones or gravel on the surface to reduce moisture loss.*

Parsley seeds or seedlings are both suitable for planting.

7 *The finished pot provides plenty of parsley for picking within a very small planted area. Pinch off flower stalks as they appear to maintain good growth.*

135

The versatility of mint

Members of the mint family are available in a wonderful variety of types and scents, but many people are afraid to grow them on account of their vigorous habit, which they fear might swamp neighboring plants. If this is a worry in your garden, you might position your mints in tubs or containers or even grow a whole range of types in a raised mint bed, where the creeping rhizomes will be contained. If you do want to plant out mint in the main garden, try restraining it by planting it in a pot or bucket before burying the container in the soil. In all cases, remember to feed and water carefully. Moving plants every few years is a good idea to avoid a build-up of disease. Most mints will enjoy some shade, and the creeping varieties make good carpet plants. It is best not to propagate mints from seed as they hybridize easily, but 6in(15cm) pieces of stem should root easily if laid horizontally about 2in(5cm) deep in moist soil in the spring. Plants will die down in winter and roots may need protecting with straw in cold areas. Fork manure compost into the bed in the fall, chopping the runners a few times with your spade to encourage good new growth the following spring. Transfer a few runners to a box of rich potting mix in a heated greenhouse for winter use.

The curled spearmint has unusual, deeply veined leaves.

Spearmint (Mentha spicata) is the most common mint.

The Corsican mint (Mentha requienii) makes a dense carpet of miniature leaves and flowers.

Black spearmint has bold purple stems and purple-tinged leaves.

Lemon mint has a fresh lemon scent, which is useful for cooking and also in cosmetics.

The buddleia mint has an upright habit and attractive soft, green foliage.

Spicy ginger mint (M. x gentilis 'Variegata') has pretty green foliage.

The pennyroyal (Mentha pulegium) prefers a damp, shady spot.

Red raripila (M. raripila rubra) has a spearmint flavor.

Creeping forms of pennyroyal make a wonderful scented carpet of small leaves.

Peppermint (M. x piperita) has a refreshing mint flavor and antiseptic properties.

Bowles apple mint has unusual thick, gray, feltlike leaves and a fresh apple scent.

Above: *An ingenious way of growing a whole collection of mints is to plant them in a variety of terracotta pots of different sizes, thus displaying their range of color, shape and texture.*

137

Chives - with a hint of onion

You can grow chives from seed or you can buy them from herb stockists. However, being a member of the onion family, perennial chives are usually propagated by dividing the bulbs and you should do this every three years in any case to regenerate the plants. Simply dig up a clump carefully and gently prize the bulbs apart before planting them out in small groups of four or five. The soil must be rich and damp, but chives are not too fussy about sun or shade. Sometimes the spiky, green, hollow leaves begin to look a little yellow and this means the soil has become too impoverished or possibly too dry. Enriching the soil with good-quality potting mixture or more conscientious watering is the answer, especially if the chives are grown in a tub or other type of container. Their spiky shape can make an effective contrast against other, leafier herbs and yet they only grow about 12in(30cm) tall, which makes them a good choice where space is limited. Snip the leaves with a knife or scissors throughout the summer to provide an interesting green garnish and a mild onion flavor to virtually any savory dish. The flowers appear in early summer - fluffy mauve pompons on the top of strong, hollow stalks. It is a good idea to nip these off despite their attractive appearance, to encourage good leaf growth.

Giant chives (Allium schoenoprasum sibiricum)

Chives (Allium schoenoprasum) *the smallest of the onion family.*

Right: *Children might enjoy growing chives in a novelty pot or container, usually made of terracotta, where the spikes and flowers make a focal point.*

Allium perutile, *the everlasting onion.*

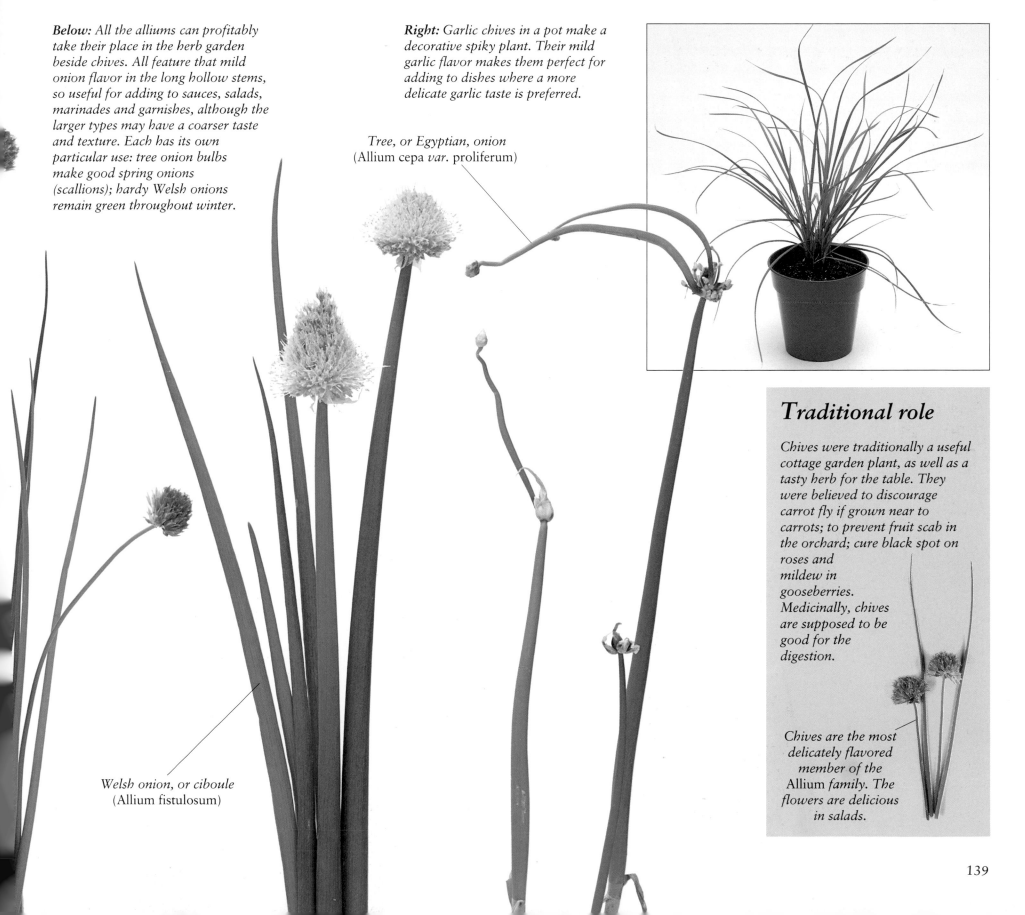

Below: *All the alliums can profitably take their place in the herb garden beside chives. All feature that mild onion flavor in the long hollow stems, so useful for adding to sauces, salads, marinades and garnishes, although the larger types may have a coarser taste and texture. Each has its own particular use: tree onion bulbs make good spring onions (scallions); hardy Welsh onions remain green throughout winter.*

Right: *Garlic chives in a pot make a decorative spiky plant. Their mild garlic flavor makes them perfect for adding to dishes where a more delicate garlic taste is preferred.*

Tree, or Egyptian, onion (Allium cepa var. proliferum)

Welsh onion, or ciboule (Allium fistulosum)

Traditional role

Chives were traditionally a useful cottage garden plant, as well as a tasty herb for the table. They were believed to discourage carrot fly if grown near to carrots; to prevent fruit scab in the orchard; cure black spot on roses and mildew in gooseberries. Medicinally, chives are supposed to be good for the digestion.

Chives are the most delicately flavored member of the Allium family. The flowers are delicious in salads.

Feathery dill and fennel

Dill and fennel cannot be grown near each other as they will cross fertilize, so unless your garden is a large one, you will have to choose between them. Both have wonderful feathery foliage that looks magnificent wherever it is planted, whether as a focal point in the herb garden or as part of a more general scheme, and it contrasts strongly with other, fleshier foliage. Neither plant dries well in the leaf, but the seeds will retain a good, warm flavor with useful sedative effects. You can use these in baking or infuse them in boiling water to make a good digestive tea or effective eyewash. Used fresh, dill leaves have a subtle aniseed aroma, perfect with fish and roast meats, while sprigs make a lovely garnish. Fennel has a much stronger flavor. Dill is a hardy annual that needs a sunny, sheltered spot. It does not transplant well, so it is a good idea to sow seeds in situ and then thin these out to about 8in(20cm) apart. Sow dill in spring if you want the seeds or at any time between spring and midsummer if you prefer to use the leaves. Fennel is a more robust perennial, reaching over 5ft(1.5m) tall and producing large umbels of yellow flowers in midsummer. There are several varieties, including a superb bronze form. The swollen base of the annual Florence fennel is used as a celerylike vegetable. Fennel can be propagated by seed in spring - thin the seedlings to 20in(50cm) apart - or by root division in the fall. Growing several plants means you can use some for their leaves and others for seed. Collect the seedheads as the seeds change color and hang them in a well-aired place to dry, with a cloth or paper bag below to catch the seeds.

Health and beauty

To make a soothing eyewash, mix one teaspoonful of fennel seeds with one of the sweetish aromatic herbs, such as roses or celandine, and about ¾ pint(400ml) of boiling water. Strain and cool before using. Make fresh each time. Fennel is popular as an ingredient in beauty products, including hair rinse (steep about 10oz/28gm of dried fennel in 1pt/550ml of boiling water and cool); it is used as a skin softener (fennel extract combined with yogurt and honey) and in toning lotions with elderflowers.

1 *When the dill plant is just 4-6in (12-15cm) tall, the foliage will be very soft and tender; trim off what you need with a pair of sharp scissors.*

2 *The soft feathery leaves will have a strong, pungent flavor and are ideal for chopping into salads and egg dishes. They also make an attractive garnish for young vegetables.*

3 *When cropping herbs for culinary use, always cut the sprigs above the point where the new leaves are developing in order to encourage the development of new growth.*

140

Above: Red fennel is an eye-catching, vigorous plant with a strong aniseed flavor. In cooking, it is the perfect partner for oily fish and aids digestion.

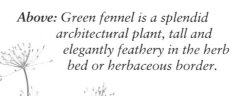

Above: Green fennel is a splendid architectural plant, tall and elegantly feathery in the herb bed or herbaceous border.

4 Once the dill has reached this size, it has become slightly coarser and a more robust kind of herb, perfect for adding to or garnishing fish dishes, such as pickled or poached salmon.

5 The mature dill plant, with its sturdy stem and flowers not quite out of bud, is used in pickles and chutneys. Its warm, spicy flavor counteracts the acidity of the vinegar.

6 Once the flowers are fully out on dill, the herb does not have such a good flavor and the texture is rather woody. It is still a useful plant for flower arranging.

Basil - a Mediterranean taste

An aromatic native of India, basil is well worth growing as an annual in cooler climates for its wonderful flavor; dried, it has a completely different taste. Basil is too tender for the general herb garden, but it may do well during the summer on a sunny, well sheltered patio with other tub-grown herbs. You could grow it under glass in a south-facing, protected corner of the garden or in the greenhouse with plenty of rich compost among the sweet peppers, eggplants and tomatoes. Regular watering and pinching out the top shoots are essential for good bushy growth. Basil is usually grown from seed in early spring to give as long a growing season as possible. Sow the seeds indoors or in a heated greenhouse and keep the potting mixture well watered. Once they are big enough, transplant the seedlings into individual pots or boxes for growing indoors or in the greenhouse. The soil should be well drained but moist, rich yet not heavy. Harvest continually during the growing season by cutting back the top and side shoots to the second pair of leaves. Left to its own devices, basil produces long spikes of white or purplish flowers from midsummer onwards.

1 Pinching out the top growth of basil is essential if you wish to create a well-shaped, bushy plant. This is best done with the fingertips.

Piquant pesto

Basil is perfect with tomatoes and most hearty savory dishes. Try chopping and steeping the leaves in oil or vinegar as a flavoring. Make pesto sauce by pounding fresh basil leaves to a pulp and mixing them with garlic, olive oil, parmesan cheese and ground pine kernels or walnuts. Use in pastas, soups or herb and garlic bread.

Below: Basil is available in a surprising variety of types and colors, from tiny-leaved Greek basil to purple forms with large crinkly leaves.

Greek basil
(Ocimum minimum
Greek variety)

Bush basil
(Ocimum minimum)

Dark opal basil
(Ocimum basilicum
purpurea)

Red/purple
ruffles basil
(Ocimum
basilicum
'Red Ruffles')

Bush basil
(Ocimum
minimum)

Sweet basil
(Ocimum
basilicum)

2 *If you pinch the stem sharply between the finger and thumb, the top set of leaves should come away cleanly and easily.*

Sweet basil (Ocimum basilicum) ready for trimming.

3 *The trimmed plant will subsequently grow from the sides to produce a well-shaped, more compact specimen. Harvest the leaves while they are still young.*

Sweet basil grows well in pots, both indoors and outside.

Anise basil (Ocimum basilicum Anise)

Ocimum basilicum 'Green Ruffles'

Sweet basil (Ocimum basilicum)

Cinnamon basil (Ocimum basilicum 'Cinnamon')

Ocimum basilicum, 'Red Ruffles'

Growing sage as a vibrant foliage plant

Most people are familiar with sage as a pungent ingredient in sausages and stuffings, but it is also a valuable garden plant with many attractive varieties. Like so many of the more aromatic herbs, sage grows wild along the Mediterranean coast and makes a shrubby plant with soft, gray-green leaves. Growing to around 24in(60cm) high, the soft feltlike foliage makes a good contrast to smaller or glossier forms, either in the herb garden or in general herbaceous borders. The spike of flowers, which usually appears in midsummer in the plant's second year, is blue, purple, pink or white and attractive to bees. Garden varieties include many beautifully colored types that are useful for coordinating and contrasting in planned planting schemes. Trimming plants back after flowering prevents them becoming leggy and unattractive and encourages good busy growth, which is particularly important if you are growing them in tubs or containers. Sages thrive in a well-drained, preferably limey, soil and plenty of sunshine. You can sow seeds in spring, but propagating by cuttings or layering is more reliable for most varieties to come true to type. Plant out established cuttings 20in(50cm) apart. Dried leaves keep their flavor well and should be collected as the flower buds begin to open. Use them sparingly with heavy, fatty food, such as pork and goose. Sage is also prized for its medicinal qualities and may be taken as a tea for headaches, a gargle for sore throats or as an aid to digestion.

Above: Trim back stems before they get leggy to produce a dense growth of foliage about 24in(60cm) high. This giant sage contrasts with other foliage shapes and colors.

Right: The wonderful array of foliage types includes creams and purples, as well as the soft 'sage green'. Variegated forms are particularly decorative.

When dried, the leaves remain aromatic.

Garden sage (Salvia officinalis) *makes a shrubby plant with soft gray-green leaves.*

S. officinalis 'tricolor' *has attractive cream-bordered leaves washed with strawberry pink.*

Red or purple sage (S. officinalis 'purpurascens') *has attractive dark foliage.*

A rich flavor

Sage has a strong flavor, ideal for rich dishes. Combined with onion, it makes a stuffing for roast meats. The Italians use it to cut the richness of calves' liver sautéed in butter; in kebabs it is threaded between chunks of lamb. Vermont sage and sage Derby cheeses are strongly flavored and bright green. Use sage in small quantities with vegetable dishes.

S. officinalis can reach a height of 12-30in(30-75cm). It keeps its flavor well when dried and leaves are best collected for this purpose in spring.

Use sage fresh or dried. When fresh, chop or tear the leaves into smaller pieces.

The midsummer flower spikes of garden sage (Salvia officinalis).

Golden sage has softly smudged green and yellow leaves.

Salvia officinalis 'rosea' has pretty pink flowers.

Attractive clary sage (Salvia sclarea) is mostly decorative.

145

Lavender as a garden feature

Bees buzzing around the erect purple stems of a spiky lavender bush are the very image of the ideal country garden. In fact, *Lavandula angustifolia* grows wild all along the Mediterranean, where the soil is dry and stony and the climate sunny but exposed. This is an excellent plant for the bed or border, where it makes a long-lived shrubby bush about 39in(1m) high. The evergreen foliage is long and narrow, gray-green and glistening with aromatic oils. The densely flowered spikes that appear in summer are purple, although there are lighter and even white forms. With its gnarled woody stems and compact habit, lavender can be grown effectively as an attractive and fragrant hedge. Choose one of the smaller varieties, such as the semi-dwarf type *Lavandula angustifolia* 'Hidcote', which grows to about 24in(60cm). For a miniature hedge to border a knot-design herb garden or small border, consider *L. nana alba*, a white-flowering dwarf form that grows to 6in(15cm) in a sheltered position. Lavender plants can be propagated in the spring or fall by rooting strong shoots of new growth about 6in(15cm) long. Transfer established plants to a well-drained, sunny position, preferably with a rather poor, stony or sandy soil. It is also a good idea to prune the bushes back a little after they have flowered to prevent them from growing thin and straggly.

One of the most popular semi-dwarf forms, L. angustifolia 'Hidcote'.

L. 'Royal Purple' is strongly scented.

L. 'Jean Davis' has tiny pale flowers.

Left: *Grow lavender near a seat or bench, where you can enjoy the sight and smell of the wonderful flower spikes at close quarters. It is the perfect companion for old roses, scented stocks, garden pinks, hyssop and thyme.*

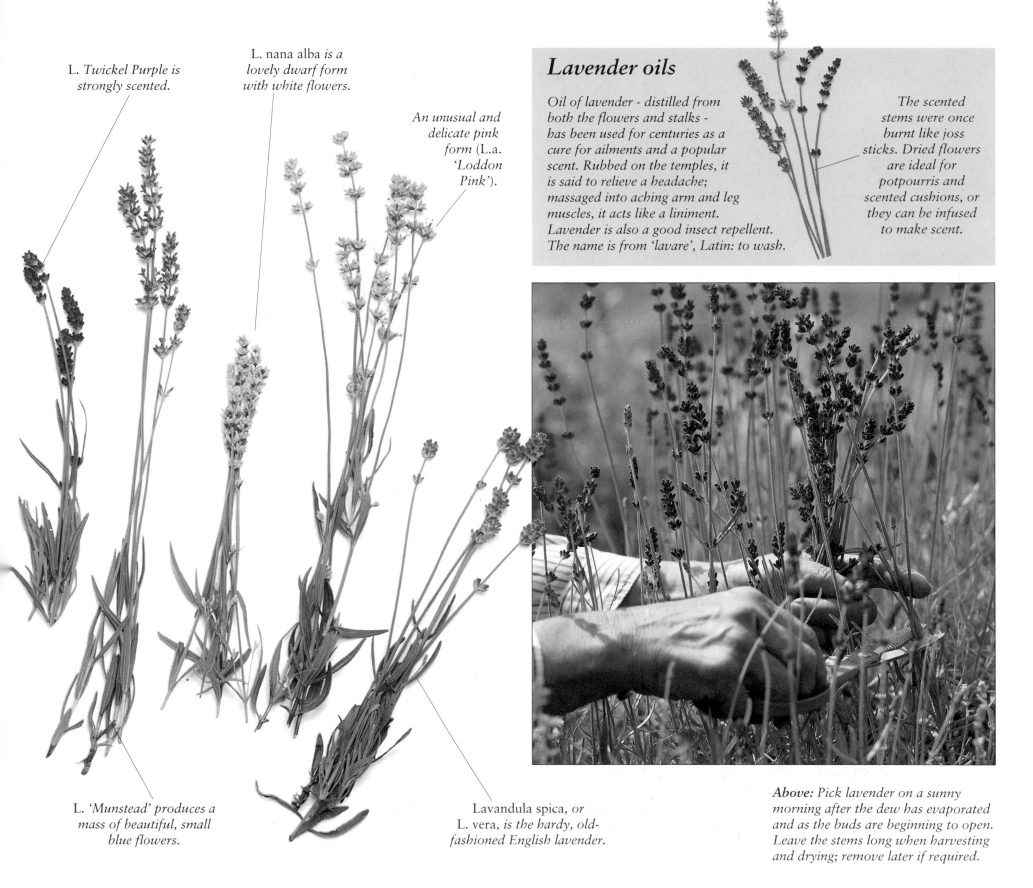

L. *Twickel Purple is strongly scented.*

L. nana alba *is a lovely dwarf form with white flowers.*

An unusual and delicate pink form (L.a. 'Loddon Pink').

Lavender oils

Oil of lavender - distilled from both the flowers and stalks - has been used for centuries as a cure for ailments and a popular scent. Rubbed on the temples, it is said to relieve a headache; massaged into aching arm and leg muscles, it acts like a liniment. Lavender is also a good insect repellent. The name is from 'lavare', Latin: to wash.

The scented stems were once burnt like joss sticks. Dried flowers are ideal for potpourris and scented cushions, or they can be infused to make scent.

L. *'Munstead' produces a mass of beautiful, small blue flowers.*

Lavandula spica, *or* L. vera, *is the hardy, old-fashioned English lavender.*

Above: *Pick lavender on a sunny morning after the dew has evaporated and as the buds are beginning to open. Leave the stems long when harvesting and drying; remove later if required.*

Comfrey as a compost crop

Russian comfrey is a large perennial plant with soft, hairy leaves, each one often as long as 30cm(12in). It prefers a rich, moist soil and a shady position. You often see it growing wild along riverbanks and in the hedgerows. It is not really suited to the smaller, more formal herb garden, but in early summer it makes a fine display in a larger one, with its stems of pink, purple or even white, bell-shaped flowers. Other variations abound. A species with cream-colored flowers called *Symphytum tuberosum* is frequently seen in northern areas of Europe and the USA. The wild, Caucasian, prickly comfrey has bright blue flowers. You can grow comfrey from seed, but propagating it by means of rooted offsets is more common, as every piece of this vigorous plant will grow into a new plant. Keeping the plants under control might be more of a problem than propagating new ones. However, there are some smaller varieties. Both roots and leaves are used medicinally, as they have good healing properties. The bruised leaves are frequently used as the main ingredient in a compress to be applied to sprains, bone injuries and bruises. It is known to help reduce swelling and encourage the healing process. This has given rise to one of comfrey's common names: knitbone. Since it is rich in minerals and grows prolifically, comfrey is a wonderful composting material and it is worth growing a few plants simply for mulching down if you have a spare corner. Comfrey leaves allowed to infuse in rainwater are also valuable as a liquid fertilizer for garden plants.

1 To make a rich compost for the garden, layer comfrey leaves with other plant material. The many layers can include vegetable waste, but avoid adding perennial weeds and roots.

Right: *You can cut the leaves, stalks and flowers of comfrey for use at any time during the active growing period. Comfrey grows rapidly and you can take several crops during the season.*

Once it is 3-4ft(90-120cm) high, cover the entire heap with a 6in (15cm) casing of soil or old compost to retain moisture and heat.

Grass cuttings

Comfrey leaves

Compost from an existing heap as a 'starter'

2 Adding a layer of grass cuttings to the compost will speed up the heating process generated by the decomposing organic material. This kills off most of the weeds.

3 A layer of rich compost and soil from the base of the old compost heap will contain lively worms and bacteria to break down woody organic matter more quickly.

How to make liquid manure

A few comfrey plants are worth growing in a corner of the garden simply for the purpose of making a powerful and nutritious liquid manure from the leaves. Infuse an armful of fresh comfrey leaves in a barrel or bin of rainwater for about four weeks and then, braving the breathtaking stench, use the liquid as a plant food. The decomposed leaves can also be used to enrich the compost heap or to fertilize your tomatoes.

Left: Large fresh comfrey leaves tucked under and around plants act as a natural mulch to retain soil moisture. As the leaves rot down, the soil will be improved and enriched.

4 Water the compost if the material seems rather dry. The compost is ready to use when the mixture becomes crumbly and dark brown and has a rich, earthy smell.

149

Companion plants

In the wild, you do not often see plants devastated by insect damage or demolished by armies of slugs and snails. Nature has its own balance of complementary plants and predators, which relies on a rich and varied but often crucial mixture of plants and wildlife. Here there is no monoculture - the kind of artificial environment we try and impose on our gardens. If you are interested in gardening as organically as possible, you should explore the possibilities of companion planting: the pairing of herbs and wild plants with your hybridized flowers and vegetables, which will ultimately enrich the precious soil and not deplete it in the way that chemical control of pests and disease does. Companion planting is believed to work through the scent of certain plants acting as a deterrent - which is why so many useful plants are herbal ones - and through exudations of the roots, which alter the nutrient and bacterial make-up of the soil. For it to work effectively, you must introduce a carefully thought-out system of mixed planting that does not have regular beds separated by paths, but considers both the needs of individual plants and their effect on the soil by rotating crops not yearly, but as each comes into season. Thus, you might see strawberries interspersed with leeks; cauliflowers with celeriac or beetroot and lettuce.

Hoverflies (left) are attracted to the vegetable garden by such herbs as fennel (shown below) and will attack aphids on nearby plants.

Pot marigolds (Calendula) - *at bottom right - are excellent companion plants in the vegetable garden. Their large root system makes them useful for planting beneath tomatoes and for making a kind of living mulch to conserve moisture. The bright golden flowers are a bonus, not only adding a splash of color between the rows, but also helping to deter aphids from beans (left) and tomatoes.*

Right: The pretty blue flowers of borage attract butterflies and bees. This makes it a good companion plant for fruits and vegetables, such as strawberries and zucchinis, helping to improve crop yields.

Cabbage white butterflies (above) are deterred from attacking cabbage leaves if there are sage plants (below) planted nearby.

Herbs as companion plants

Herbs are not only beautiful - they are useful garden plants. Every plant in the garden affects the plants around it. It may be just by the large leaves offering shade and protection to more delicate plants. Some herbs deter pests and many attract beneficial insects that are valuable pollinators or act as predators of common garden pests.

The most common plant combinations are:

Borage, thyme and hyssop	attract bees which improve crop yield in strawberries and other fruit.
Chamomile	has been found to repel insect attacks, thus improving crop yields.
Chives	have a reputation for preventing black spot on leaves and deterring aphids.
Dill and fennel	attract hoverflies, which then go to work on aphids.
Garlic	with its strong odor is thought to be beneficial to roses.
Mint	especially the Pennyroyals have been found to be good fly and midge repellents.
Rosemary and thyme	mask the scent of carrots, which deters the carrot fly.
Sage	repels the cabbage white butterfly.
Nasturtium	has an excellent and interesting reputation as a companion plant. It keeps pests away from the vegetable garden, partly owing to the way it attracts aphids away from them. Nasturtium has also been found to repel ants and whitefly. It provides good ground cover and young leaves and flowers are delicious in salads.
Pot marigold	is a good all-round and attractive companion plant in the vegetable garden. It grows freely, is self-seeding and deters nematodes in the soil.

Planting a bay tree

Most people think of bay as an attractive, shrubby evergreen bush or as a highly decorative standard tree sporting a pompon of glossy green leaves on top of a single slender stem. The leaves are the main attraction, being large, shiny, deep green and highly aromatic. They can be picked and used at any time, but dry well too, the flavor actually strengthening and becoming more mellow. They are used extensively in cooking - in bouquet garnis, stocks, stews and marinades. Native to the Mediterranean, this handsome laurel is susceptible to frosts, so may even need protection in warm climates. In cooler ones, it is a good idea to plant the bay in a tub for overwintering in the greenhouse or conservatory. It does not grow well from seed so is usually propagated from cuttings, best taken in early summer. Bay prefers a light, well-drained soil, but grows slowly even in sunny, sheltered conditions. This makes it expensive to buy as a mature plant, but an excellent herb for trimming and clipping into formal shapes.

1 Good drainage is essential, so add a few crocks in the bottom of the pot - it is worth saving any pieces of broken plant pot for this purpose.

2 Start filling the container with a light, sterilized soil. Synthetic particles are available to improve drainage. Make sure that the pot has been scrubbed and sterilized, too.

3 Take the bay out of its pot and lower it gently into the new container, holding the stem gently between your fingers and supporting the foliage against your hand.

Make sure that the bay is planted at the same depth as it was in its original container.

4 *When the plant is in place, continue filling the pot with more of the soil, taking care that the bay remains upright and in the correct position. Try to avoid getting any soil on the foliage.*

Do not fill the pot right to the rim, but leave some space at the top to allow for watering

6 *Stand the finished pot in a sunny, well-sheltered spot and bring it under cover at the first signs of frost. Bay produces small yellow-green flowers in late spring or early summer, followed by black berries.*

5 *A layer of small stones or gravel on the surface of the soil not only helps to retain moisture, but also looks attractive. In addition, it discourages weed growth.*

Bay looks particularly good in a Mediterranean-style terracotta container.

153

Creating a herb garden for the windowsill

A windowbox is the perfect way to grow a selection of culinary herbs in the minimum of space. The kitchen windowsill is an obvious site, providing the window opens conveniently enough for regular access to your mini garden. Make absolutely sure that the windowbox is firmly secured; use strong brackets or ties and check these periodically for wear or weathering. The box might be home-made from new or old timber, painted to match window frames or shutters; or it might be lightweight plastic, antique stone or terracotta. If the windows are too exposed a site, why not plant up an indoor windowbox, perfect for a few of the more tender species, such as basil. Regular cropping or trimming is important to ensure that the herbs remain small and leafy. Keep the box adequately watered and apply a liquid feed during the growing and cropping season. The soil soon runs out of essential nutrients in the confines of a box, especially where plants grow prolifically and where rain washes constantly through the soil. A mulch of small pebbles conserves moisture and reduces the effect of heavy rains.

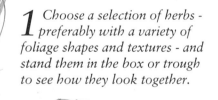

1 Choose a selection of herbs - preferably with a variety of foliage shapes and textures - and stand them in the box or trough to see how they look together.

2 Take out the plants again and arrange a few crocks or broken pieces of pot in the bottom to prevent the potting mixture washing away.

3 Add 2-6in(5-15cm) of washed gravel or pea shingle to make a well-draining layer at the bottom of the box. Top up with planting mix.

4 Plant the herbs, keeping to your original plan and maintaining a balance of appearance, height and habit. Tip them gently out of their pots and into your hand, supporting the stem lightly between your fingers.

5 Top up with soil, making sure it settles between the plants without any air gaps. Do not fill right to the top of the box to allow for watering.

6 A sprinkling of gravel or small stones on top of the soil around the plants looks attractive and helps to slow down moisture loss.

Herbs in the kitchen

The flavor of fresh herbs is far more delicate than that of dried ones, so use them generously. Generally speaking, add them at the end of cooking for maximum effect. Mint, basil and tarragon change their flavor once dried, so do not expect them to taste the same as before. Add fresh, chopped herbs with a swirl of cream to home-made soups; sprinkle them on salads; tie them in tiny bundles to add to stocks and stews; or tuck sprigs of rosemary, sage or thyme under the roast joint with a slice of unpeeled onion and a clove of garlic to bring out the flavor.

Chives (Allium schoenoprasum)

Culinary thyme (Thymus vulgaris)

Sorrel (Rumex acetosa)

Sage (Salvia officinalis)

French tarragon (Artemisia dracunculus)

Parsley (Petroselinum crispum)

Oregano (Origanum vulgare)

7 The finished trough looks good and includes a useful blend of flavors for the cook. If you use plenty of herbs in cooking, reduce the number of plants in the box to two or three bigger plants.

155

Freezing herbs

We are so familiar with the idea of drying herbs to preserve them that we often forget that most of them can be stored very successfully in the freezer. In fact, for some herbs, such as parsley, basil and tarragon, freezing is by far the best option, as their flavor changes quite dramatically when they are dried. Frozen herbs can be chopped and added to soups, stews, marinades, sauces - in fact to any dish - but they cannot be used as a garnish. Pick the herbs fresh and sort them out to remove any dead or withered parts. Then arrange them in sprigs. You need not blanch them, but give them a quick rinse in cold water and dry them on kitchen paper or a clean tea towel to remove any small insects. Freeze them in small quantities, making sure the bags are well labeled. For convenience, you may like to put together some useful combinations, such as a bouquet garni mix or, say, parsley, chives and tarragon for adding to egg or fish dishes. To use the herbs, chop them in their frozen state as soon as you remove them from the freezer. Instead of freezing herbal mixtures in sprigs, you could chop them finely together and freeze them in ice cubes to pop into stews and sauces. Herb flowers, such as borage, can be frozen in the same way for adding to drinks.

2 *Combine the chopped herbs and sprinkle a little of the mixture into each compartment of the ice cube tray. You may need extra trays if you are freezing large quantities.*

Marjoram

Thyme

Parsley

Sage

1 *Herb mixtures frozen in ice cube trays are so convenient for adding to stews, soups and sauces at any time of year. First chop the herbs finely with a sharp knife or herb mill.*

Herb flowers in ice

Some herb flowers, such as borage and salad burnet, are traditionally added to summer drinks. Freeze the flowers in filtered or bottled water; chemically treated tapwater tends to go cloudy when frozen.

3 *Top up the container, ideally with filtered or bottled water, and place the tray in the freezer. The herb cubes will remain usable for several months.*

Freezing individual fresh herbs

Freeze individual herbs in small sprigs. When you are ready to use them, shred them off the stem while they are still frozen.

1 *Gather the herbs and lightly wash the trimmed sprigs in clean water to remove any dirt or small insects.*

2 *Absorb any excess moisture by patting the sprigs gently with a piece of kitchen paper or a clean tea towel.*

3 *Package the herbs ready for freezing in individual plastic bags. Squeeze out as much air as possible, fasten and label clearly.*

Drying herbs

Although it is possible to grow a few of the more compact herb varieties in pots on the windowsill to carry you through the winter, this will rarely keep pace with demand if you are a keen herb user. Drying your own herbs enables you to continue using them all year. However, some herbs are simply not worth drying; evergreens, such as thyme, for example, should be fine for cropping right through the winter, while parsley, chervil and fennel simply do not dry well, losing all their flavor in the process. Drying herbs is quite simple. When you have harvested and sorted them, just tie them in bunches and hang them in any shady but warm and well-ventilated place, such as an attic or shed. The quicker the herbs are dried, the better the color and flavor and the less chance there will be of them going musty. Some people use a well-ventilated airing cupboard successfully or dry herbs in a cool oven with the door ajar. Another traditional method is to use a drying cupboard, where the herbs are set out on meshed trays. This is a useful strategy for flowerheads. It is also possible to buy an electrical version for quicker and more predictable results. Once the herbs are dried, strip the leaves from the stems and store them in airtight containers. To dry seeds, collect the seedheads just before they ripen and dry them in bunches upside down with a cloth or paper below to catch any seeds that fall. Strip the rest of the seedheads from the stalk and leave them to dry out completely for another week or so before storing.

Lemon balm

Santolina

Rosemary

1 *Gather your chosen herbs for drying and lay the sprigs or branches all facing the same way. Tie the stalks together loosely into small bunches with string, twine or cotton.*

2 Hang the bunches to dry in a warm, airy place away from direct sunlight. A barn or attic is ideal. The bunches should hang freely or they will take too long to dry and become dusty.

Santolina   Rosemary   Lemon balm

3 When the herbs are dry, shred them off the stalks, taking care not to crumble them too much or they will not retain so much flavor. Some leaves, such as bay, can be stored whole.

4 Store the dried herbs in glass or ceramic jars with tight-fitting lids. Label them clearly and keep them away from direct light. Replace dried herbs every twelve months.

Dried herbs around the home

Dried herbs are useful when fresh ones are not available, particularly those that do dry successfully, such as rosemary, sage, thyme, mint and lemon balm. Some, such as fennel, dill, cumin and coriander, are better when the seeds are dried and stored. Remember that dried herbs have a more intense flavor than fresh ones, so you will only need a pinch or a teaspoonful, rather than a bunch of leaves. Dried herbs also make refreshing herbal teas and household products, such as mothbags and small scented bags. Scented dried herbs include lavender, clove carnation, roses, santolina, scented pelargoniums, bergamot and woodruff.

Part Four

GROWING FLOWERS

The beauty of a kitchen garden is that you can simply step outside and pick the freshest vegetables, fruit and herbs. And while you are gathering these choice ingredients, why not pick a few flowers to decorate the table? One of the joys of flowers in the kitchen garden is being able to cut blooms for the house. If you use a lot of cut flowers, it is a good idea to grow a few rows of popular annuals, such as sweet peas and 'Ostrich Plume' asters, in the vegetable garden, where they can be cut heavily without spoiling the look of a flower garden. Alternatively, you may prefer to grow your flowers in more traditional borders. Although some flowers are specially recommended for arranging, most flowers can be cut - some simply last longer than others. Since long straight stems and perfect blooms are desirable for cutting, it pays to take particular care with growing techniques. Keep borders free of competing weeds and take regular precautions against slugs and snails. Feed plants regularly and water them in dry spells. To help the soil retain moisture and create good growing conditions, mulch between perennial plants with well-rotted organic manure in spring and fork plenty more into the soil where annuals are to be grown. Use supports for tall plants early on, before the stems start to bend or droop, and place 'cage'-type plant frames over herbaceous plants in spring when growth begins. Tie delphinium stems individually to canes with raffia. Push pea sticks or canes in with groups of tall, weak-stemmed annuals and surround dahlia and chrysanthemum plants with three or four stakes around which to weave a network of strings to provide support.

Left: Vibrant flowers in a kitchen garden border. **Right:** *Visual harmony in yellow, orange and red.*

Instant gardening using annuals

For instant color almost anywhere, annuals are the answer. They are the simple solution for the new homeowner who wants a garden in a hurry, or for making an existing garden look its best for a special occasion. They are good for filling odd gaps in a border, for planting up containers and perfect for a balcony, patio or pathway. Annuals can also be used creatively in traditional knot gardens - or for Victorian-style carpet bedding schemes now enjoying a revival. They are also good value for planting in beds of their own where you need a splash of color that will last all summer. Use annuals in informal 'random-look' cottage-style planting schemes, or in formal beds edged with straight rows of flowers and blocks of color broken up by occasional 'dot' plants - perhaps standard fuchsias. However, annual beds are a lot of work, so do not take on more than you can comfortably manage. Plants can be grown from seed on warm windowsills indoors, or bought ready to plant from garden centers in early summer, just as they are coming into flower. Do not plant them out until after the last frost. Annuals need good soil and a sunny situation with reasonable shelter to do well. To keep plants flowering continuously they need frequent attention - watering, feeding and deadheading regularly. Since the plants do not survive freezing, pull them out in the fall and replace them with spring bulbs or winter and early spring bedding, to avoid leaving the beds empty.

Above: *Use annuals to fill a narrow bed that would soon be overcrowded if planted with perennials. These are antirrhinums, tuberous begonias, lobelia and dwarf African marigolds.*

Right: *A colorful knot garden using* Impatiens *to fill in the intricate patterns created by dwarf box hedges; A useful scheme for a shady spot as both kinds of plants are shade-tolerant.*

162

Annuals in containers

Tubs, troughs and hanging baskets are the perfect way of decorating a patio and for adding eye-catching detail to special places all around the garden. Favorite plants include pelargoniums, fuchsias, begonias and lobelias, but almost any compact or trailing annual is suitable. Most annuals are sun lovers and need direct sun for at least half the day. Begonia semperflorens, Impatiens and fuchsias will flower in light shade if they are in flower when planted. The best time to plant up containers is in early summer, just after the last frost. Fill the pots with any good potting mix, remove the plants from their containers and plant them close together so that the pots look well filled from the start. Containers need daily watering; allow the potting mix to take up as much water as it can.

Right: *A pot of* Begonia semperflorens *will be a blaze of color all summer. It can be easily moved to different spots and looks good on an outdoor table, too.*

Below: *Large containers suit a bold, mixed planting scheme. Here, verbena, pelargoniums and African marigolds make a striking and colorful display.*

Above: *Hardy annuals (*Nigella, Calendula *marigolds and cornflowers) grown by the 'sow where they are to grow' method, make a distinct pattern in the floral carpet covering the bed.*

163

1 Prepare the soil over the entire bed some time in advance of planting. Dig a hole for each plant about twice the size of its rootball.

2 Put the excavated soil next to the hole, ready for filling in around the roots once the plant is in place.

3 Put a spadeful of well-rotted manure or other organic matter in the hole and mix well. Add more manure to the excavated soil.

Planting a perennial

Perennial plants will stay in the same ground for two to four years, so it is vital to spend time on soil preparation before planting. Tackle soil pests with a soil insecticide or dig the ground several times in winter to expose pests to the birds. Dig in as much bulky organic matter as possible, sprinkle a general fertilizer evenly over the soil and rake it in shortly before planting. Perennial plants are traditionally planted in fall or early spring, but since they are dormant at that time, you may prefer to delay planting until mid-spring when some growth is visible. Buying pot-grown plants enables you to add new plants in summer when they are in full flower, but they will need generous watering during dry spells for the rest of that season to allow the roots to establish. Herbaceous perennials spread to form dense, congested clumps, with unproductive old material in the center and young flowering shoots only around the edge. After two to four years, split up the clump and throw away all the old exhausted central parts, leaving only young material, divided into fist-sized sections, to be replanted. The best time to do this is in early spring, just before the new flush of growth starts. A few of the more rugged types, such as michaelmas daisies, can be divided in the fall when the last flowers are over, but bearded irises need to be lifted and divided in summer, about six weeks after the flowers are over. Take this opportunity to improve the soil again before replanting and be sure to replant the clumps at the same depth as before. This is important: herbaceous peonies, for example, will not flower if their crown is planted more than 1in(2.5cm) below the soil surface, and bearded iris need planting so that the top half of each horizontal rhizome is above ground or they will suffer from the same problem.

4 Sprinkle a handful of general purpose fertilizer into the hole and mix well with the soil. Add half a handful of fertilizer to the pile of soil alongside the hole and, again, mix well.

5 Tip the plant gently out of its pot (knock the base of the pot sharply against something solid if the plant is difficult to dislodge). Slide the plant out without breaking up the rootball.

6 Lift the plant by its rootball into the hole. Do not handle the plant by its stems. The top of the rootball should lie roughly level with the soil surface. Rotate the plant until its best side faces the front of the bed.

7 Surround the rootball with the improved soil excavated from the planting hole, and firm it lightly down. Add more soil to bring it up to the level of the surrounding bed.

8 Water well in, trickling water around the edge of the root-ball. Mulch with 1-2in (2.5-5cm) of rotted organic matter or bark chips and keep well watered.

Using spring bulbs

Spring bulbs are highly versatile flowers, and useful for bold splashes of early color all round the garden. Naturalize them permanently in borders and lawns, on banks, and as colorful carpets under trees and shrubs, or use them as temporary spring bedding plants in containers or in formal borders. Some kinds of bulbs are better for one type of use than another. Tulips are best taken out of the ground and stored 'dry' for the summer, as they rot easily if left in the ground. This makes them particularly suitable for formal uses. Dig the bulbs up after the foliage has died down naturally, rub the soil off and keep them in a cool, dark, dry place till replanting time in the fall. Daffodils, *Anemone blanda* and many other popular bulbs prefer to be left undisturbed once planted, so they are better for naturalizing. Clumps of naturalized bulbs only need to be dug up and divided when they have become so overcrowded that they no longer flower well - in this case do so when the foliage dies down after flowering, or you may have difficulty finding them. In mixed borders, plant large leafy bulbs such as daffodils towards the middle of the border, with clump-forming summer herbaceous flowers, such as hardy cranesbill, as a 'screen' in front of them - these will be growing up as the daffodil foliage is dying down. Alternatively, grow small early flowering daffodils, such as 'February Gold', that have less foliage and die down earlier.

Daffodil

Hyacinth

Crocus

Iris reticulata

Pushkinia

Anemone coronaria 'De Caen'

Ornithogalum

Allium

Left: Viridiflora *tulips, planted with white wallflowers against a background of interesting foliage shapes and textures, make a very attractive green and white cameo.*

Tulip

Anemone blanda

Chionodoxa

Muscari

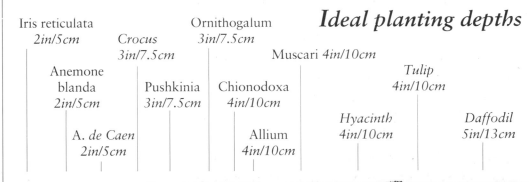

1 If you want to create a natural effect, the easy way to plant bulbs is to scatter them randomly over the area to be planted and then to plant them where they fall.

2 In the case of large bulbs, make holes and plant to the correct depth. With small bulbs, such as anemone, which have no right way up, press them in with your finger.

Above: *Anemone coronaria 'De Caen' is a favorite spring-flowering bulb that grows about 8in(20cm) tall. Plant in groups for best effect. The flowers are also good for cutting.*

Right: *Most people plant bulbs far too shallowly. As a rough guide, cover the bulbs with twice their own depth of soil (measured from tip to base).*

Ideal planting depths

Iris reticulata
2in/5cm

Ornithogalum
3in/7.5cm

Crocus
3in/7.5cm

Muscari 4in/10cm

Anemone
blanda
2in/5cm

Pushkinia
3in/7.5cm

Chionodoxa
4in/10cm

Tulip
4in/10cm

A. de Caen
2in/5cm

Allium
4in/10cm

Hyacinth
4in/10cm

Daffodil
5in/13cm

Planning a spring border

After a long dull winter, the first spring flowers are always welcome, but instead of just dotting them around the garden, make them into more of a spectacle by concentrating them together in a spring border. This does not have to be an isolated feature that looks dull for the rest of the year - spring plants can be happily integrated into a summer border, where they provide the starting point for a long season of color. Plan the border so that there is a good balance between spring and summer flowers - the foliage of spring flowers will provide a leafy 'foil' for those that follow on later. Plant tall summer flowers, such as delphiniums, towards the back of the border; spring kinds tend to be low-growing, so plant them towards the front. Low bulbs, such as *Anemone blanda,* make a colorful carpet under shrubs and towards the front of the border, while taller kinds, such as daffodils, are best kept in clumps towards the middle, where the untidy foliage will be partly hidden by other plants. Buy pots of spring annuals, such as polyanthus, colored primroses and forget-me-not, already in flower, to fill any odd gaps. In a large garden where there is room, you could create a spring 'cameo' purely from early flowers, which makes a much more solid effect. It also gives you a chance to create interesting plant associations based around favorite plants, such as euphorbias, *Epimedium* and hellebores. For a specially striking yellow trio, try *Euphorbia wulfenii,* narcissi and the early yellow *Paeonia mlokosewitschii.*

Cheiranthus 'Bowles Mauve'

Dicentra formosa

Bergenia 'Ballawley'

Primula denticulata

Doronicum orientale (leopard's bane)

Dicentra spectabilis 'Alba'

Primula rosea 'Grandiflora'

Above: *Forget-me-nots, with bluebells, tulips,* Helleborus orientalis *and* Dicentra spectabilis *'Alba'.*

Above: *Daffodils and* Helleborus foetidus *(stinking hellebore) make a successful plant association. Despite its name, the hellebore does not smell unpleasant unless leaves are damaged.*

Above: Paeonia mlokosewitschii *is a beautiful early-flowering species, which for obvious reasons is better known by its common name of 'Mollie the Witch'.*

Above: Euphorbia wulfenii *has striking lime green spring flowers. This is a canary yellow form of it called 'Lambrook's Gold', which must be propagated from cuttings.*

Narcissus
'*Hawera*'

Primula vulgaris
flore-plena
'*Dawn Ansell*'

Ranunculus
(*turban buttercup*)

Primula
vulgaris
(*cultivated
primrose*)

Hyacinths

Pansies

Primula rosea

Tulip '*Orange Nassau*'

Viola '*Prince Henry*'

Summer-flowering bulbs

If you mention bulbs, most people think of spring-flowering daffodils and tulips, but there are plenty of less well-known kinds that flower in summer. Some, such as gladioli, acidanthera, *Eucomis* (pineapple flower), tuberous begonia and tigridia, are not hardy enough to leave in the ground through the winter, so plant them in spring. In the fall, when the flowers are over and the foliage dies down, dig them up, dry them off and store them in a frost-free place. Summer-flowering bulbs that can be planted permanently in a mild climate include summer hyacinths *(Galtonia)*, which have large sprays of greenish white flowers similar to those of yucca, and *Crinum powellii*, the giant of the summer bulbs. Each one has a long thick neck that must remain above ground when it is planted. Give it rich soil. A hot, sunny, flower bed at the foot of a wall is the best place to grow nerine and *Amaryllis hippeastrum* (not to be confused with the indoor plant *Hippeastrum*). Both like to be planted and then left undisturbed, without other plants around them to prevent the bulbs ripening properly. The flowers appear in late summer or fall on bare stems, after the leaves have died down. All summer bulbs need a sunny sheltered spot and well-drained soil to thrive. Prepare the soil well before planting, by forking in a handful of general fertilizer per square yard, and plenty of well-rotted organic matter - coir is ideal for summer bulbs, as it improves the soil structure without holding too much moisture. Summer bulbs are not always readily available in garden centers - in case of difficulty, buy mail order from a specialist bulb catalog.

1 *To plant a canna, choose a pot large enough to take the roots with ease. Part fill it with potting mix and rest the tuber on the surface, allowing for 2in(5cm) of mix above the tip.*

Galtonia candicans
(summer hyacinth)

Large-flowered gladiolus

Canna *'Lucifer'*

Eucomis bicolor

Acidanthera murielae

Tigridia pavonia

Miniature Gladiolus orchidiolus

2 Cover the tuber with more potting mix and then fill the pot almost to the rim. Tap the pot down firmly to consolidate the potting mixture.

3 Leave a 1in(2.5cm) gap between the surface of the potting mix and the rim of the pot for watering. Water until the soil is evenly wet; allow any surplus to drain away.

4 Keep the pot in a slightly heated greenhouse or sunroom or on a sunny windowsill until there is no danger of frost. Then you can safely put it outdoors.

Repot as necessary. An established canna makes a large plant that needs a 10in(25cm)-pot or even more.

Ideal planting depths

Miniature Gladiolus (3in/7.5cm)

Acidanthera (6in/15cm)

Eucomis (4in/10cm)

Tigridia (2in/5cm)

Galtonia (6in/15cm,

Large-flowered Gladiolus (4in/10cm)

Canna (2in/5cm)

Right: A canna planted in a pot will not grow as tall as it would in a border. Expect flowers in mid- to late summer. If kept well fed, the tuber will be larger the following year and may produce more than one flower spike.

Canna in a pot

If you grow summer-flowering bulbs in pots in a frost-free place, they will start to flower earlier than dormant bulbs planted straight into the garden soil. Canna is a particularly good plant to grow in this way, as it makes a good summer pot plant for the patio; you can also plunge the pot to the rim in a bed of annuals as a 'dot' plant.

Charming sweet peas

Left: Sweet peas can make a striking feature, as here in a terracotta pot, with plants trained to climb up a rustic wigwam of loosely interwoven willow wands.

Sweet peas are surprisingly versatile traditional favorites. They are good both as cut flowers and garden plants. Grow them up a 'tent' of twiggy pea sticks to give height to a border, or as climbers on trellis or netting. Knee-high dwarf cultivars can be grown in hanging baskets, and as low-flowering summer 'hedges', edging lawns or borders. Any sweet peas can be cut for indoors - the more you cut, the more flowers are produced. However, sweet peas that have been allowed to ramble freely often have short, kinked or bent stems. If you want sweet peas with long straight stems for cutting, grow them as cordons. Here, each plant is trained individually up a cane as a single stem, secured with plant rings or raffia. Nip out the thin curly tendrils between thumb and finger, otherwise they 'grab' hold of the flower stems, making them kink. Seed catalogs list a huge range of different named varieties of sweet peas and mixtures are also available. Not all varieties are well perfumed, so check the descriptions. Old-fashioned cultivars, such as 'Painted Lady' and the various old-fashioned mixtures that are sometimes available, are best in this respect. Their flowers are not as large as in the modern, wavy-edged, Spencer types, but their scent makes up for it. Even if you do not cut sweet peas for the house, remove deadheads at least once a week, otherwise the plants quickly stop flowering.

1 *Sow sweet pea seeds spaced 1.5in (3.75cm) square in a tray filled with seed sowing mixture. You can sow the seeds in early fall for early flowers, but spring is the usual time for sowing them.*

2 *Push each seed into the sowing mixture until it just disappears below the surface. The seeds should be buried to their own depth in the sowing mixture.*

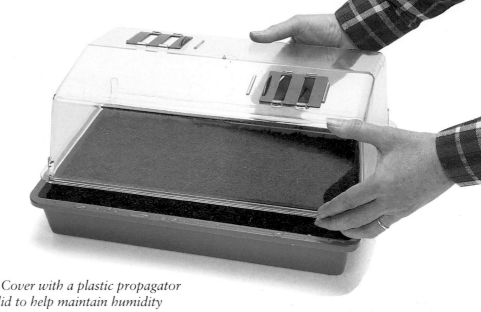

3 *Pinch the sowing mix together over the top of each seed to fill the hole. If necessary, sprinkle a fine layer of extra sowing mix over the surface.*

4 *Water thoroughly and let surplus moisture drain away. Large seeds absorb a great deal of water before germinating so check the soil regularly.*

5 *Cover with a plastic propagator lid to help maintain humidity during germination. When the first shoots appear, slide back the vents.*

Above: *A flowering sweet pea hedge, produced by spacing plants about 12in(30cm) apart and training them up a post and netting fence. Regular cutting encourages new buds.*

Left: *Sweet peas hold themselves up to trellis or netting using their tendrils, but these also tangle together and catch on neighboring flower stems, making them bend or kink.*

6 *Remove the lid entirely when the shoots are 1in(2.5cm) high. Gradually acclimatize the plants to harder conditions by standing them outside when the weather is fine.*

You can easily remove the growing tip by nipping it out between thumb and forefinger.

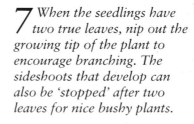

7 *When the seedlings have two true leaves, nip out the growing tip of the plant to encourage branching. The sideshoots that develop can also be 'stopped' after two leaves for nice bushy plants.*

Dazzling dahlias

1 *Choose a pot large enough to take the dahlia tuber with room to spare and half fill it with potting mixture. Sit the tuber in the middle.*

2 *Cover the tuber with 2in(5cm) of potting mix, filling the pot almost to the rim. Tap the pot down sharply to consolidate the potting mix.*

3 *Water and put in a frost-free place. When the first shoots are 3-4in(7.5-10cm) tall, you can remove a few to use as cuttings if you wish.*

After a long spell out of fashion, dahlias are back in favor again. They make superb free-flowering plants for midsummer to fall displays, but their large, distinctive flowers can easily overpower more delicate neighbors, so they need placing with care. Plant them in groups among spring and early summer-flowering shrubs to brighten up the border later in the year or keep them to a bed of their own. Dahlia flowers are wonderful for cutting, and the more you pick, the more you get. Named varieties are available with flowers ranging from tiny to gigantic, and from neat pompon shapes to open-faced collarettes and spiky-petaled cactus types, in virtually every color except true blue. Dahlias are grown from tubers planted out in late spring, about two weeks before the last frost. A small selection is available in garden centers as dry tubers in spring, but enthusiasts send for catalogs from specialist nurseries or order plants at flower shows in late summer. Rooted cuttings are occasionally available in spring, but do not plant these out until after the last frost. Dahlias need moist, rich soil in a sunny spot and some regular attention for best results. Plants continue flowering right up to the first fall frosts. In mild areas with free-draining soil, some people can get away with leaving dahlia tubers in the ground over the winter, protecting the tubers under a deep layer of leaf litter. Elsewhere, lift and store them (see panel).

Right: Compact dahlias make good plants for the front of a border, but they are also good grown in pots - try them on a patio, or plunged to their rims to fill late gaps in borders.

Lifting and storing dahlia tubers

Leave plants in the ground until early frosts start to blacken the foliage. Cut the stems down to 6in(15cm) and dig the plants up carefully to avoid damaging the tubers. Turn them upside down so that the sap can drain out of the hollow stems. When they are completely dry, rub any soil off the tubers. Store them in a dry, frost-free shed, away from rodents. Check the tubers regularly, and if you see any rot, cut out the affected area and dust the cut surface with yellow or green horticultural sulfur.

1 To grow dahlias in a border, dig a hole into well-prepared soil, about 8in(20cm) deep and wide enough to take the tuber with space to spare.

2 Place the tuber on top of a small mound of soil in the bottom of the hole, and space the roots out so that they make good contact with the soil.

3 Hammer in a strong stake just behind the tuber. If you leave this till later you risk damaging the tuber. Cover the tuber and fill the hole.

Above: The tip of the tuber should be 6in(15cm) below the ground. If a late frost threatens the first shoots, cover them with bracken or peat.

Right: Dahlias make good cut flowers. Shake them lightly to dislodge any earwigs and put the stems into water immediately after cutting them.

Cut dahlias when there are plenty of tight petals in the center of the bloom for longest vase life. Stand them in deep tepid water.

Cactus-flowered dahlias are characterized by quilted petals.

Remove lower leaves before arranging or they make the water slimy.

Top up the water in vases daily, as dahlias are heavy drinkers.

175

Cottage garden borders

Nowadays, many people with modern houses have a cottage garden. The popular 'recipe' includes roses round the door, hollyhocks at the gate, flowers mixed with vegetables, fruit trees instead of flowering shrubs, and no lawn but gravel paths edged with flowers or low lavender hedges everywhere. However, most people today want at least a small lawn, and vegetables grown amongst flowers are never as productive as when grown in rows in a proper vegetable garden. The real secret of a successful cottage garden is to have carpets of plants covering the borders so that no soil is visible, and to grow plants that look 'cottagey' even if they are not entirely authentic. Old-fashioned annuals, such as godetia, wallflowers, snapdragons, clarkia and alyssum, can be allowed to seed themselves about randomly - simply pull up any that grow where they are not wanted. Rampant spreading plants like golden rod, lemon balm *(Melissa officinalis)* and many of the herbaceous campanulas can be grouped in a bed of their own and left to fight for space. These are useful for creating a low-maintenance cottage garden, although the result can be a little on the wild side for many people's liking.

Above: *A plain picket fence and old-fashioned flowers such as these snapdragons create an unsophisticated feeling of 'olde worlde' charm.*

Left: *When you mention cottage gardens, this is what immediately springs to mind: riotous borders overflowing with a huge mixture of flowers apparently fighting for space.*

Other cottage styles

As an alternative, try beds of roses underplanted with low carpeting herbaceous flowers, with tall delphiniums, tree mallow and thalictrum growing through towards the back. Enthusiasts also find room for choice cottage 'treasures', such as gold-laced polyanthus, old-fashioned pinks and auriculas, which need special care to thrive.

Right: Many wildflowers are old cottage garden plants. Obtain seeds from specialist suppliers; do not take plants or seeds from the wild.

Popular plants for cottage gardens

Astrantia
Aquilegia
Crown imperials
Cultivated primroses
Daffodils
Forget-me-not
Hardy fuchsia
Honeysuckle
Lavender
Myrtle
Nasturtium
Pinks
Pulmonaria
Pyrethrum
Rosemary
Old-fashioned roses
Sedum acre (stonecrop)
Sempervivum arachnoideum
(cobwebbed houseleek)
Sweet william, Wallflowers

Above: Traditionally, the front gardens of old cottages did not have a lawn, but were completely filled with a carpet of flowers, leaving just a path to the door.

Right: Hardy cranesbills, mallows, roses and lady's mantle are all at home in a cottage garden. Rejuvenate clumps of perennial plants every few years.

Scented foliage

Herbs
Lavender
Salvia grahamii
(blackcurrant scent)
Salvia rutilans *(pineapple scent)*
Scented-leaved pelargoniums
(various citrus, spice, balsam,
rose and pine scents)

Scented borders

Scent is one of the most overlooked assets of a flower garden, yet by choosing carefully it is possible to have a constantly changing perfumed accompaniment to a walk round the garden. Seating areas are particularly good places for perfumed plants, or they could be used as the inspiration for an entire fragrant garden. Scented plants come in two basic types; those with perfumed flowers and those with aromatic leaves. Choose some of each for a succession of scents. Flowers deliver their perfume all the time they are fully open and some, such as lilies, only last a short time. Some of the best scented flowers have the most uninteresting blooms - you would hardly notice night-scented stock and sweet rocket, so tuck them in with more spectacular but unscented displays. Modern cultivars of old scented favorites, such as flowering tobacco and many roses, have lost much of their scent - choose old-fashioned kinds where possible. Use fragrant flowers in distinct groups all round the garden, so that their scents do not overlap. Aromatic leaves need to be bruised to release their fragrance, so place them where you can brush past them. Since scent is easily dispersed on the breeze, choose a sheltered, preferably enclosed, site for scented plants. Although many plants are scented during the day, most produce their strongest scent in the evening to attract night-flying insects for pollination. Scent will also be strongest when the air is warm and humid.

Below: Herbs and roses - a cottagey combination chosen for scents and colors. The herbal scents are released when the leaves are brushed, so plant herbs towards the front of the border.

Above: Not all roses are heavily perfumed, but one of the best is this 'Fragrant Cloud', a hybrid tea. Check rose catalogs for details of other well-scented kinds.

Scented flowers

Cosmos atrosanguineus
(chocolate-scented cosmos)
Dianthus *(pinks)*
Hesperis matronalis
(sweet rocket)
Honeysuckle, Hyacinths
Jasminum officinale *(Jasmine)*
Lavender, Lilium regale,
candidum *and some lily hybrids*
Nicotiana affinis
(flowering tobacco)
Night-scented stock
Roses, Stocks
(Brompton or East Lothian)
Sweet peas
Wallflowers

Above: Nicotiana alata *is well known for scenting the evening garden. Few modern varieties are strongly scented; try 'Fragrant Cloud' and the tall* Nicotiana sylvestris; *both white.*

Above: *Pinks and lavenders; both the foliage and flowers of lavender are scented; this cultivar is a form of French lavender with large petals,* Lavandula stoechas *'Pendunculata'*

Right: Santolina chamaecyparissus (cotton lavender) has silvery foliage that smells attractively herbal when bruised. Victorian ladies brushed their clothes with it to repel moths.

A rose border

Nurseries and garden centers now stock a wider selection of roses than ever. Modern bush roses flower from early summer until the fall, and include the hybrid teas and floribundas, also known as large-flowered and cluster-flowered roses. Miniature roses grow to about 12-24in(30-60cm) tall, while patio roses are about halfway in size between miniature and bush roses, and ideal for containers. Ground cover roses are prostrate, but it is difficult to weed around them, as their stems are so prickly. However, grown on upright stems as short standards, they are spectacular, creating a waterfall of flowers. Old-fashioned shrub roses are grown for their classic scent and charming old-world colors. They are bush roses but often a bit straggly and in need of support; most only flower in early summer though some kinds have occasional flowers later too. Nowadays, some modern roses, such as the New English roses) are bred to look like old roses but with the long flowering season of modern kinds - the best of both worlds. Traditionally, roses were grown in beds of their own with bare soil underneath, while modern bush roses look good grown with a carpet of annual flowers. Old-fashioned roses look best treated like any flowering shrubs and grown in a mixed border of cottage garden flowers or herbaceous plants, particularly those that flower after the roses are over.

Left: Herbs are good for the front of a border of roses where the soil gets dry. Here, 'Graham Thomas', one of the New English roses, teams effectively with the purple-leaved sage.

Left: Standard and half-standard roses add height to a border without taking up too much space. This is Rosa 'Excelsa', a once-flowering rambler that can attain a height of 20ft(6m).

Below: Modern roses are all too rarely used as flowering shrubs in mixed borders. Here, 'Masquerade', a floribunda, mingles with Campanula, Alchemilla and other border plants.

Left: Arches or pillars are useful for accommodating climbing roses, such as 'Veilchenblau' and 'Compte de Chambord', shown here, and help to make the border look tall and solid.

Below: Miniature roses are often mistaken for houseplants, but they are outdoor varieties and require the same care as their larger cousins. This red variety is called 'Royal Baby'.

Left: Violets make superb ground cover under roses, as they thrive in light shade and do not compete for nutrients. This old moss rose, 'Jean Bodin', is planted with Viola cornuta. Violets self-seed readily, and soon create their own carpet. Plant them 1in(2.5cm) apart.

Index to Plants

Page numbers in **bold** indicate major text references. Page numbers in *italics* indicate captions and annotations to photographs. Other text entries are shown in normal type.

Right: *An informal herb garden where a splendid scented patchwork of plants almost smothers a winding path of stepping stones and completely disguises the garden's underlying. rectangular shape.*

Credits

The majority of the photographs featured in this book have been taken by Neil Sutherland and are © Colour Library-Books. The publishers wish to thank the following photographers for providing additional photographs, credited here by page number and position on the page, i.e. (B)Bottom, (T)Top, (C)Center, (BL)Bottom left, etc.

A-Z Botanical Photographic Collection: 162(B Michael R. Chandler)

Peter Blackburne-Maze: 69(inset BR,CR,CB), 70(TR), 71(BL,BR), 72(TL,CL), 92(BR), 93(BL), 97(TC,TR), 98(T), 99(TR,BL,BR)

Pat Brindley: 167(TR), 179(BR)

Eric Crichton: Credits page(L), Second contents page(BR), 14, 19(CR,BR), 23(BR), 30(BL), 32(BL,BR), 41(BR), 51(TL), 53(L,TR), 54(TR), 71(TL,TR), 80(BR), 83(BR), 93(CL), 98(B), 99(TC), 162(TR), 173(CL,BL), 178(BL,CB), 179(TR), 181(TL)

John Feltwell (Wildlife Matters): 150(T © Sheila Apps), 151(TL)

John Glover: Half-title page, Credits page(R), 19(TR), 39(TL), 43(BR), 80(BC), 81(TR), 100, 106(BL), 107(B), 110(TR), 111(T), 129(B), 130(BC), 141(TL), 146(BL), 150(BL,BR), 151(TC,B), 160, 163(TL,CR), 176, 177, 181(R)

Natural Image: 180(L, Bob Gibbons), 180(BR, Liz Gibbons)

Clive Nichols: 163(BR), 166(BL), 168(BL), 169(TL,TC,TR), 172(L), 174(BR), 179(L, Designer: Wendy Francis), 180(TR)

Photos Horticultural Picture Library: 42(TR), 43(TR), 55(TL), 81(BL), 97(BL), 181(B)

Acknowledgments

The publishers would like to thank the following people and organizations for their help during the preparation of this book: The Royal Horticultural Society Garden at Wisley, Surrey; Brinsbury College - The West Sussex College of Agriculture and Horticulture; John Nash and Sally Cave at Costrong Farm, West Sussex; Lynn Hutton at Secrets Farm Shop, Surrey; The National Institute of Agricultural Botany, Cambridge; Murrells Nursery, West Sussex. Rosemary and David Titterington, Marian and everyone at Iden Croft Herbs for their help and patience during the photography sessions. Thanks are also due to Cadmore Lodge Hotel near Tenbury Wells, Worcestershire for providing space for photography. Country Gardens at Chichester for providing plants and photographic facilities. Thanks are particularly due to Cherry Burton and Sue Davey for their enthusiastic help and guidance. The publishers would also like to acknowledge the following owners and designers: Mrs. Sally Treganowan, Mrs. R.R. Merton, Mr. Peter Herbert.